Barbed Wit
and
Malicious Humor

PATRICK MAHONY

BARBED

WIT

&

MALICIOUS

HUMOR

THE INSTITUTE FOR THE STUDY OF MAN
Washington, D.C.

ISBN 0-941694-12-7

First Edition, 1956
First *Institute for the Study of Man* Edition, 1983

To the Memory of my Mother,

Mrs. E.C. Bliss

ABOUT THE AUTHOR

Patrick F.H. Mahony was born in England in the year 1911, the son of a British Army officer who was killed in action during World War I, shortly after winning a citation for bravery. Mr. Mahony's widowed mother subsequently married an American citizen and brought her children to the United States of America, where they grew up in the pleasant atmosphere of Santa Barbara, California.

Reared in this stimulating social environment, the young Patrick Mahony had ample opportunity to observe the social behavior of prominent members of American and European society. Becoming a regular contributor to a wide range of American newspapers and journals, he soon developed that profound insight into human nature which is clearly revealed in the over two hundred articles, ten books, and various stage plays and operatic libretti which he produced in the course of his life.

Nowhere is Mr. Mahony's subtle comprehension of the sharp and sardonic repartee which arises so frequently from the interface of self-opinionated but intelligent personalities better portrayed than in *Barbed Wit and Malicious Humor*. However, notwithstanding the title of the book, the more serious and authentic anecdotes are freely interspersed with a plenitude of more lighthearted, (if somewhat apocryphal) humor, and when the last page is reached, and the pleasant task of reading is completed, we find that we have learned to share something of the author's deep love of humanity, and that we have become more closely endeared to our fellow beings because of, rather than in spite of, their petty failings.

Patrick Mahony's own adult life was spent — when not engaged on the lecture tours which took him repeatedly around America and Europe — in the social milieu of Los Angeles and, more particularly, Hollywood. Here, in his attractive home nestled on the slopes of a steep Hollywood canyon, he took particular pride in hosting small but intellectually stimulating soirees, attended by guests carefully selected from a broad cross-section of writers, poets, actors and actresses — many of world renown. Those who had the privilege of enjoying his hospitality will always remember him as a gracious host, who was blessed not only by the quality of courtesy and consideration but also by those same skills as a raconteur which reveal themselves with such impressive clarity in the pages of this highly entertaining book.

Introduction

What is humor? The dictionary says that it is a changing state of mind. Which is about all one could expect from a dictionary. For surely humor defies analysis. Wit is different again in that it implies a swift perception of the incongruous, but I prefer to use the word in the sense of what the French call *pointe*.

The oddest thing of all about either wit or humor is why one person may laugh at a given joke and the funniness be completely overlooked by another. In my opinion, a course in "Humorology" ought to be on the curriculum of every college and university, because a knowledge of it forms an important part of human psychology. Humor has something to do with getting outside of ourselves and can often have its context in deep tragedy, as in Bernard Shaw's *Saint Joan* and the Fool in *King Lear*. Actually, life's tragedies are frequently charged with humor; hence there are touches of pathos in this book.

It is essentially a collection of sarcasms, insults, rapid-fire repartee, clever retorts and epigrams by the famous over a long period. Such things are often thrown out to test men's moods, serving frequently as subtle and penetrating touchstones of the mind. Is it not significant that today doctors of the mind see a psychiatric remedy in the use of sarcastic repartee, which they feel is a blessed safety valve?

To some readers unflattering stories about certain people normally surrounded by an aura of greatness will seem nothing less than sacrilegious. My book proves that many of them possess the prowess to fling insults most expertly. Would that they applied themselves to the Art of Pleasing with such diligence! But my own experience has taught me that the so-called celebrity is as wild a ragout as ever escaped from any cook book. Most of the famous people I have known have had their feet planted firmly in mid-air.

Many readers will wonder how it happens to be me who has spent the endless hours of research necessary for preparing a book of this kind. Most of my books have concerned themselves with profound and serious subjects, mostly of a metaphysical nature.

The answer is that I have come to the conclusion that life is far too serious to be taken seriously! I may say also that I have found comedy much harder to write than tragedy, which may be due to the fact that people laugh in several different ways, and usually cry in only one.

The basic note of this book is one of aloof entertainment. I have lately observed that the modern reading public, ruthless in its search for variety, is amused by hearing of the blows rained upon others. They can dip into this volume and be invigorated by the refreshing spectacle of their favorite, or most disliked, public figure being pilloried!

I am indebted to many people in many ways, above all to the courteous staff of that wonderful institution called the New York Public Library. Most of these anecdotes, however, have not seen the light before. Some I have overheard at dinner parties, or from sleuthing around important grapevines. Every anecdote is of necessity the memory of a memory, and is usually embroidered in the telling from person to person.

Famous people soon become inured to the use and abuse of their names in funny stories and are forced to waive a certain amount of privacy. In doing my research I have noticed that certain good stories have done duty from age to age, being grafted on a more topically famous personality to lend current interest. This, I take it, is the story-teller's license and I have not tried, therefore, to give every story a birth certificate.

A few will be recognized as having passed into the "folk tradition" of anecdote. But to those superior people who fling at me the word "chestnut," I will wish them a worse fate in the Next World than they would ordinarily deserve!

PATRICK MAHONY

Contents

... 1

Literary Larking

Perhaps the inherent seriousness of writers has, through a sense of contrast, stimulated the nimble exercise of wit on the part of their profession in general.

At any rate, the prolific supply of good stories in this field has become proverbial. Horace Greeley, for instance, was as famed for his hot temper as for the excellent way he edited the New York *Tribune*—also as the possessor of the most indecipherable longhand.

It was said that when he once wrote a note of dismissal for an unsatisfactory clerk, it was used in three illegitimate ways. First, the young man presented it as a testimonial for another job and got himself accepted. Then, with the same letter, he obtained a prescription for some medicine from a chemist shop. Later he found it was acceptable as a free pass on the New York Central Railroad.

Be that as it may not, there was only one compositor on the *Tribune* who could decipher Greeley's copy. One day, as a joke, the man's fellow compositors decided to experiment with a remarkable ruse. They caught a couple of pigeons when he was out to lunch and inked their claws. Then they allowed the birds to make numerous scattered markings on several sheets of paper.

These were placed on the desk of the expert in Greeley's longhand, who began setting type from them upon his return. Everything seemed to be going well until he came to a particularly wild splash. It was a real piece of abracadabra and for some minutes he sat trying to figure it out. Finally, in desperation, he went to see Greeley.

"You've got me this time, Mr. Greeley," he said, looking very puzzled. "This paragraph stumps me." And he pointed at some of the inky claw-marks.

Greeley looked at the paper, read the "writing" for a moment and then thundered, "Blockhead! What's the matter with you? Do you expect me to print it myself? Here, I'll rewrite the whole page."

Besides possessing untidy writing, some writers have a poor sense of personal tidiness. Rudyard Kipling was one who carried this failing to the point of harshness.

He lived very retired, always anxious to avoid the public. One lazy summer afternoon he was reclining in a comfortable chair enjoying the seclusion of his garden at Burwash in Sussex. Suddenly he was taken by surprise, when an American woman admirer of his work, who had entered by climbing over the wall, appeared before him. Kipling let fall the book he was reading, made a grimace of displeasure, and pulled himself together.

"Oh, Mr. Kipling!" the woman pleaded. "I wanted so much to have a glimpse of you, but I never knew you'd look like this!"

Kipling raised himself from his chair indignantly. "The fact is Madame, I *don't* look like this. You have caught me on one of my off-days."

If this great poet happens to be sleeping through the present generation, he will surely have a renascence in the next. There was, for instance, a Los Angeles school girl who was asked by her teacher what she thought of Kipling. The reply was shattering. She said:

"I don't know. I've never kippled."

In the period of his fame, admirers of Kipling would go to great lengths to obtain his autograph. Often checks which he wrote for smaller sums would not be cashed. One fan, eager to obtain the coveted autograph, wrote to him thus:

"I have read that you make five shillings a word in your writing. I herewith enclose my autograph book attached to which is a P.O. for ten shillings. Please fill in and return."

Kipling wrote two words, as instructed, in the space assigned for him: "Thank you!"

Lord Tennyson was another great poet who was not very generous with his autograph. He was noticed for his eccentricities and seemed to believe that a writer had to behave as if he were half-mad to be considered a genius. Even before he had acquired a modicum of fame with his fine poetry, his personality was replete with mannerisms.

A brother of the poet was a very average type of man with little or no predilection towards literature. One autumn they went to France together on their summer holidays. They spent a few nights at a hotel in one of the French provinces and the servants, including the hall porter, were amazed at Tennyson's undisciplined conduct. Not knowing that he was a poet, they more than likely put him down as a mental case in the charge of his nurse.

To make matters worse, Tennyson could speak no French, but his brother had a sometime knowledge of the language. One morning the brother came downstairs early for a before-breakfast walk. On the way out he noticed that the fire in the lobby grate was dying. He called this to the attention of the hall porter, saying:

"Prenez garde, de ne pas laisser sortir le feu (Watch the fire; Don't let it go out)." But instead of pronouncing *feu* (which means fire) correctly, he accidentally said *fou*, which means fool.

So when Tennyson himself appeared sometime later he was apprehended and not allowed to leave the hotel. The mistaken instructions had clinched the hall porter's suspicion that Tennyson was an escaped lunatic.

As a mature poet, Tennyson did not lose any of his eccentricity.

He was known to walk out of a social gathering or turn his back on an old friend over an imagined slight. Coventry Patmore, an English poet of stature, has put on record the occasion when Tennyson and he were discussing a forthcoming book of poems. The two men were talking about the matter over a glass of sherry, which happened to be an inferior brand.

"If I were you, Tennyson," said Patmore, having read one of the poems aloud, "I wouldn't publish that one. It isn't up to your standard."

Raising himself to his great height, Tennyson walked to the fireplace, threw the contents of his glass into the flames, which hissed back at him, and walked towards the door, shouting: "And this damnable sherry isn't up to my standard, either!"

A more formal critic, Professor Churton Collins, who was an eminent scholar of classical renown, suggested in a book he wrote that Tennyson owed a debt to the classics which he had never acknowledged. Later Tennyson met him at a gathering of litterateurs, and flung at him: "You're a louse in the lock of literature."

Such sarcasm can only be compared to a literary predecessor of Lord Tennyson, Dr. Samuel Johnson. He regarded Boswell as an intolerable bore and would try to think of every device to rid himself of his volunteer henchman.

Once he left a note for Boswell at a restaurant where they were to foregather.

"Don't bother to look for me," the message read. "I have gone to commit suicide."

But the persistent Boswell caught up with his idol, finding him enjoying beer and sausages somewhere else before a crackling fire.

"I think I will defer my experiment until next week," he offered by way of explanation.

Always ready with advice to young writers, he suggested to a young man who asked permission to dedicate his new book to him that, instead, he inscribe it thus:

"To the great reading public. May it buy this book in quantity and bring me reward."

However, to another who asked his opinion of his book in manuscript form he said: "This ought to be sent to the House of Correction."

Which brings to mind a story told about Elinor Glyn, mother of the sex novel, and the writer who made the word "It" synonymous with sex.

Like many literary tyros at the commencement of their careers, Mrs. Glyn had difficulty in losing the virginity of being unpublished. To one magazine editor she sent a note with her ms. which ran:

"Would you please publish the enclosed manuscript or return it without delay, as I have other irons in the fire."

The editor read the material, attached a rejection slip to it, and scribbled:

"Put this with your other irons."

How he must have recriminated later on when the books of Elinor Glyn sold in the millions!

After her success it became the fashion to smile at the mention of her name, for the product of her pen was tawdry compared with what she could have accomplished. She had an astute mind and could have done work of much better quality if she had thought it would have sold as well—which of course it wouldn't.

Elinor Glyn knew all the important people of her day—statesmen, artists, musicians and writers—and while none of the writers admired her work, they all envied her success.

Being born beautiful, she never failed to fascinate a bachelor, and Henry James was no exception. He liked her very much personally, but could not resist firing a subtle shaft at her on one occasion. Elinor was not too happy about her latest book, and told James her feelings when they met at a dinner party.

"Oh, it's selling all right," she said, "and the royalties are streaming in. But I feel it is not me at my best. This book has something lacking . . ."

James, who was then literary arbiter of London, knew that Mrs. Glyn was fishing for a compliment; and although in a debonair mood, he could not bring himself to say what he did not really feel.

"Actually, Mrs. Glyn," he said, "I have not read one of your books *in toto*. But I did thumb through the copy of your latest endeavor which you kindly sent to me. I think you are wrong. You write as well as ever you did."

Mrs. Glyn purred contentedly and began flattering James upon the value of his words, when suddenly he threw his stiletto: "As regards your opinion of your book, Mrs. Glyn, it is possible that your taste is improving?"

So celebrated was Mrs. Glyn that even a piece of doggerel was composed about her:

> Would you like to sin,
> With Elinor Glyn
> On a tiger skin?
> Or would you prefer
> To err with her
> On some other fur?

To her credit Elinor Glyn loved America and readily claimed it as her largest reading public. Another egregious female novelist named Ouida avowed a cult of hatred against everything American. At a party, she was talking to Chauncey Depew and somehow was not aware that he was the great American wit and legislator. She noticed an American couple in another part of the room and made a gesture of displeasure.

"Take me into the next room, Mr. Depew," she said with a snobbish toss of the head. "There are some of those nasty Americans over there."

Later in the evening Depew got even with her. The same

American couple passed by and Depew caught her arm, as if to save her from danger.

"Look out, Madame Ouida," he said abruptly. "There are those Americans again who buy your nasty books."

Why is it, I wonder, that when a European author's books sell well in America, he so often holds a grudge, instead of being grateful? Vicente Blasco Ibáñez achieved a great success with his *Four Horsemen of the Apocalypse* in this country, later becoming famous all over the world. Yet he fulminated against America because his next book did not receive the same hospitality as his first. It was perhaps due to the title that the second book failed, for he insisted upon the somewhat unfelicitous *Mare Nostrum*, which means "Our Sea".

One day in New York City he was treated to the following conversation in a hotel lobby:

"Have you read the new book by Ibáñez?"

"No. What's it called?"

"*Mare Nostrum* or something like that."

"What in Hell does that mean?"

"Something to do with horses, I suppose."

After overhearing this, the Spanish novelist blew a gasket and took the next ship home.

Mercifully, there are a few foreign writers who have appreciated American favors, and James Joyce was one of these. He always spoke and wrote about the United States in the highest terms. And perhaps by way of reciprocity there happen to be a larger number of James Joyce societies here than anywhere else in the world. (There is not even *one* in Ireland!)

Joyce alienated himself from his native land where he suffered nothing but poverty and where his now world-famous books were proscribed. But Dublin is still the storehouse for the best stories about him, and every summer the town is filled with students of his work who go there to find material for their theses upon the great writer.

In his early struggle for a living he became an usher in a Dublin cinema, but prior to that job he had held a job as a messenger. The story is told about an interview he once had with a crusty bank manager to whom he was applying for a vacant position. The man catechized the youthful Joyce thus:

"Do you smoke?"

"No."

"Do you drink?"

"No."

"Do you go with girls?"

"No."

And the manager threw up his hands. "Away with you! You'd probably rob the bank."

During this unhappy period of struggle, Joyce spent a few weeks in Cork City, working at a temporary job. And, through the merest accident, I happened to meet some years ago the landlady at whose lodging house he had stayed at this time. To a student of Joyce this would indeed have been a piece of literary treasure-trove. But I was more interested in obtaining from the good lady an anecdote or two. Could she recall anything amusing about the great writer?

The lady was now rising eighty, and her memory, therefore, was probably not infallible. She dug into it as deeply as she could.

"Always short of money, he was," she said. "And his health none too good. A delicate sort of young fellow . . ."

"Is it possible," I asked, "that you can remember anything in particular that he said—something funny?"

"Never said anything funny," she continued. "A sad type of person, you know. He was laid up a few days here, that I do recall."

"Just a cold, no doubt?" I asked.

"No," said the woman, her eyes brightening, "an attack of fluency."

Of course she meant influenza, but those who have tried to read

Joyce's *Ulysses*, with its disordered syntax, will read something more into her mistake.

Later on, when his reputation as a writer began to spread about the literary grapevine of Dublin, Joyce was requested to call upon an editor with a view to his doing some book reviews.

"You know, Joyce," said the editor patronizingly, "there are so many candidates for this kind of work. Why, I only have to put my head out of this window and whistle. In one or two minutes there will be a couple of writers clamoring to do reviews for me!"

"To review what?" asked Joyce, as he raised a twitting finger, "your head?"

Is it any wonder that he left Ireland, the home of so many unhappy memories, and joined his expatriate Irish friends in Paris? Here, at least, starvation was not so humiliating and gradually recognition came to him.

A Dublin friend called upon him at his flat in the Quartier Latin and was struck by the many native symbols. Everything spelled Dublin, from the pictures on the walls to the souvenir ash tray and cigarette box. Even a large rug on the floor portrayed the winding course of the River Liffey flowing through its beloved city.

The friend expressed surprise at all this nationalism, since Joyce had apparently left Ireland, never to return.

"How come," he asked, "that you bring Dublin to Paris like this?"

Joyce's face lit up with an impish smile.

"There was once an English Queen," he said slowly, "who died with the word 'Calais' written upon her heart. When I die, 'Dublin' will be found on mine."

No one can deny that James Joyce brought about an alteration in literary style, just as Picasso influenced the changes in art. And among the first of the American writers to join the Joycean cult was Ernest Hemingway, who seems to have hitched his wagon to the right star.

As readers of this famous writer know, Hemingway finds it necessary to use certain words in his books which are frowned upon in polite society. An editor of one of his early books objected to this sort of thing in his manuscript and requested that certain four-letter words in the text be deleted.

Hemingway pretended not to understand what words the editor was referring to, knowing that he was a puritanical type of man, and wishing to pull his leg. So the editor, not wanting to enunciate the offensive word, took a memorandum pad and wrote it down, handing the pad to Hemingway. After a short discussion Hemingway agreed to the deletion and the two men went out to have some luncheon.

In the middle of the meal the editor clapped his hand to his forehead in a gesture of horror.

"My God!" he cried. "I wrote down that word on the pad which my secretary always checks during the noon hour. I must go back to my office and destroy the page. It's headed: 'Things to do to-day.' "

Another writer who leaves very little unsaid in his books is the Frenchman Jean Paul Sartre. The Left Bank of Paris is usually buzzing with stories about this witty writer. It is said that he sent a scenario manuscript to a Hollywood film studio, and in due course he received back the script accompanied by a rejection slip.

Evidently it was thought that he had talent for this type of writing, because he was advised that the studio would like to see something else, but that his present submission did not measure up to the prerequisites of a good film story. For his information these were: religious sentiment, dramatic surprise, human interest, brevity, and, last but not least, sex appeal.

Sartre took this well-meant counsel under advisement and penned a reply to the studio secretary.

"How would this do?" he queried. " 'My God!' cried the Duchess, 'let go my leg!' "

If one thinks about it, this sentence contains all the ingredients for the so-called model film story, but it sounds more like a line out of an Oscar Wilde play!

Oddly enough we find Oscar at his Wildest when he was undergoing the ordeal of his criminal trial. After his conviction, he made one of his finest witticisms. He was being escorted to Reading Gaol along with a group of felons to whom he was shackled. They were standing on an open railway station in charge of a warder. It was raining hard and the warder possessed the only umbrella. Wilde and his fellow prisoners were getting soaked to the skin.

"If this is the way Queen Victoria treats her convicts," protested Oscar, "she doesn't deserve to have any."

As a ready wit he stood alone, petted, yet feared, by society. He stigmatized *Debrett's Baronetage of England* as "the best thing in English fiction ever written." And he said of a certain titled lady who, after the demise of her husband, dyed her hair blonde: "Grief has turned her fair."

While the editor of a fashionable magazine for women, he could not resist a thrust at the ridiculous changes of taste. Referring to a new mode of dress, he suggested: "With this creation, the mouth should be worn slightly open."

No one managed to take down Wilde while he was in a position of command—except his friend Sarah Bernhardt. They were together once, rehearsing one of his plays, when a serious disagreement took place between them as to the way the part should be played. In order to clear the air, Wilde said: "Do you mind if I smoke, Madame?"

And the Divine Sarah's answer fell like stones: "I don't care if you burn."

Smoking was one of Wilde's inveterate habits. Once when dining at the house of a dowager who would not allow smoking within her presence, a candle-lamp began smouldering.

"Please put out the lamp, Mr. Wilde. It's smoking," said she.

"Certainly, Madame," said Wilde. "But what a happy lamp!"

Wilde got his first name from his godfather, King Oscar of Sweden, and was not, as some writers have mooted, named after a figure in Irish mythology by his mother, who studied that subject deeply. Actually he was prouder of his middle name which was O'Flaherty, whose prefix, "O," designated his family as being aristocratic in the Irish sense. As he himself declared, he always *owed* everybody!

Poor, tragic, wonderful Oscar Wilde died "beyond his means." When asked where he would be buried, made his last witticism: "It doesn't matter. Posterity will find me."

The subject of cemeteries brings to my mind the image of Bernard Shaw. I once interviewed him at his home at Ayot St. Lawrence, near London, and he informed me that he had settled there because he had checked on the life span of the graveyard inmates at all the places which suggested themselves for residence within a short radius of London. And the headstones at the Ayot St. Lawrence cemetery proved that this district was the ideal one for longevity!

I was prepared to find a misanthropic old man, but to me he was courteous and kind. I told him of my admiration for his dramaturgy.

"Not many people seem to have grasped the fact," he said slowly in the thick brogue which clothed his speech, "that my plays begin where they end and end where they begin."

And then, fastening his basilisk eyes upon me, he continued in the kindliest way: "Oh, Patrick, you're Irish and will get everything wrong that I tell you. Much better that I write the interview for you. Sit here and talk to Charlotte."

So saying, he went to his desk and I found myself talking to Mrs. Shaw, mostly about her great husband.

"He's got a mind like radium," she said proudly. "Can one analyze radium?"

Tactlessly I asked her how she had managed to keep at bay the women who had thrown themselves at Shaw. She smiled knowingly:

"According to rumor, my husband has broken many hearts. After we were married there was an actress who pursued him. She threatened suicide if she were not allowed to see my husband . . ."

"And did she die of a broken heart?" I asked.

Shaw interrupted, leaving his desk and waving a few pages of foolscap.

"Yes, she did," he said gleefully. "Fifty years later! Now, Patrick, here is what I want to have you tell your lecture audiences about me. I have written it all down so that you can memorize it word for word. And after I have gone hence, you can sell these pages for fifty pounds." (There he was wrong; I got only ten for it!)

My only other meeting with this extraordinary being was in Piccadilly some years later. I spied him in his checkered suit strolling along at a sprightly gait—he was then perhaps eighty-five. Who could resist a few words with him? I sidled up to his moving figure.

"Mr. Shaw," I said, "I haven't seen you for so long!"

And his reply bodied forth without demur: "Have you tried?"

On the occasion of his ninetieth birthday I sent him a golden shamrock, which I purchased in Dublin, to which he fired back with one of his famous postcards: "I shall wear it until I myself drop off of it."

My friend, Maurice Maeterlinck, and Shaw once exchanged words sharply in the newspapers. Shaw called Maeterlinck "the joy of every parodist." To which the Belgian dramatist replied: "Shaw is like an old chateau, not even haunted by a spirit."

Surely each man had equally as much to offer the world; Maeterlinck to the life of the spirit, and Shaw to the world of the intellect.

During his wartime exile (he was a refugee from the Nazis), I worked with Maurice Maeterlinck on magazine articles. He was unable to understand the technique of magazine article writing, and I became his assistant. He was, of course, first and foremost a dramatist, and his best known work is *The Blue Bird*, which is, I think, a perfect prism onto which will ever shine the light of truth.

The world-wide success of this play led several manufacturers and persons in trade to adopt the name of it, and a curiously funny thing happened to Maeterlinck and myself one day. I was taking the master out to luncheon and as we were about to step off the curb at the Plaza Hotel, a woman approached us holding out her hand.

Thinking she was a fan, Maeterlinck took hold of it. And to my horror the lady said: "Mr. Maeterlinck, I have just been told who you are, and I must tell you how much I am enjoying my Blue Bird washing machine."

Since Maeterlinck did not understand English, he smiled courteously and looked at me for a translation. Needless to say, I did not transpose her words into French. Instead I told him that she was asking the way to Madison Avenue.

"Then why did she go off in the wrong direction?" he asked naively.

Maeterlinck's life came under the microscope in the days of his great fame. In his youth he fell in love with a beautiful French actress named Georgette Le Blanc and the romance lasted twenty years. When it came to an end, an astonished public learned that he had married, at the age of sixty, a young woman of nineteen.

All the world wondered what had happened to his much-publicized romance with Georgette Le Blanc and an American journalist, who happened to be in Nice, decided to find out the truth.

Knowing that Maeterlinck seldom granted interviews, she stormed the famous writer's fabulous Villa d'Orlamonde overlooking the Mediterranean, where he lived in seclusion with his new wife. The journalist sent in a card on which she penned the following:

"I am an American writer in great difficulties. If I can do an interview on you for my paper I can pay my passage home, and all will be well. If not, my only alternative will be to commit suicide."

How could Maeterlinck or anyone else refuse to grant such a request? In due course the news-hen was admitted to his presence. She posed her first question in a nervous voice: "May I ask why you left Georgette Le Blanc?"

Maeterlinck rose from his chair, flung a fierce glance at her, and snarled: "Go and commit suicide, Madame."

In English literature the personality of Henry James suggests itself as a comparison with Maeterlinck. He was as shy and retiring, lived the same cloistered existence, and was beloved by all who knew him. He possessed a poor sense of humor and relied on funny stories told by others. So when he met Mark Twain, he realized that he was at a loss. He began telling a literary anecdote, a hardy survivor from a remote past, asking if the American humorist had heard it. Mark shook his head and Henry James continued, but broke off.

"Are you sure you haven't heard this story?" he asked.

"Quite sure," said Mark. "Go right ahead."

James took up the thread again but before reaching the climax, he noticed a smile of recognition on Mark's face and asked again: "Are you really sure you haven't heard it?"

Mark Twain's face creased into a broad grin.

"I can lie once," he said, "and I can lie twice for courtesy's sake. But there I draw the line; I can't lie again. Yes. I have heard the story. In fact I invented it myself!"

Henry James was very generous about giving his books away to his friends and on a certain occasion gave a rare copy of one book, duly autographed, to George Eliot, the renowned woman writer. One day he happened to be visiting her and George Henry

Lewes, her husband. As he was leaving, he asked if he could borrow the book, since it was now unobtainable.

The absent-minded Mr. Lewes had put the book aside with several others and went to get it just as Henry James was settling himself down in his carriage. Imagine his chagrin when George Henry Lewes came out of the house with a stack of books, saying: "I don't know which one is yours, but I know it's one of these. Pray keep all of them for we've no use for them. For heaven's sake, don't return them."

Which brings to mind a similar experience of Bernard Shaw. While browsing in a secondhand book shop he came across a presentation copy of one of his own books peeping at him from amongst the dusty shelves. He bought it for a shilling and returned it to the person for whom he had originally autographed it, inscribing the flyleaf: "With renewed compliments of Bernard Shaw."

He was just as terse in dealing with an ambitious society matron who wished to show him off at one of her parties. She had never met Shaw, but saw no harm in sending him a formal invitation which read: "Lady So-and-So will be at home on such-and-such a day."

Shaw just returned the card, adding: "Mr. Bernard Shaw will be likewise!"

In Ireland this sort of deviltry would be ascribed to the "Irish Imp" inside him. George Moore, the author of many fine novels, possessed this ingredient in full measure. He would spare no one the piercing of his stiletto tongue, not even William Butler Yeats, who said of him: "George Moore has no enemies, but his friends don't like him."

Yeats, who was deified in his own lifetime, had one failing. He curried favor with the titled, especially the English aristocracy. This worried his friends no end, because they regarded him as the poetic spokesman for the Irish Nationalist cause.

At one time, Yeats even flirted with the possibility of accepting

a knighthood, which prompted Moore to suggest that the Nation-
alists take out insurance against the risk with Lloyd's!

Actually, Yeats came of a good middle-class Anglo-Irish family
and was the son of an artist, who in turn was the son of a clergyman. But he preened himself falsely on being related to a noble
family, the Butlers of Ormonde.

During a house-party at Coole Castle, the home of his friend,
Lady Gregory, he and George Moore were among the guests. Yeats
began dreaming aloud about his noble ancestry.

"Do you know, George," he said to Moore, "by rights I should
be the Duke of Ormonde!"

Moore raised his eyebrows, then fired a broadside: "What was
the name of your father, Willie?"

However, Yeats got the last laugh on Moore. A year or so later,
Yeats was visiting Moore in his London home. One morning they
set out together on a literary pilgrimage to see the grave of Oliver
Goldsmith.

Meeting a friend in the street they spoke of their mission and
the man remarked that it would be a pleasant outing.

"How much more pleasant it would be," said Yeats, "to be visiting the home of Goldsmith and going to see the grave of George
Moore."

Yeats' secret dislike of Moore continued beyond the grave. He
used to tell a story of the conversation which he overheard in the
village near Moore Hall in County Mayo, just prior to the funeral
of the famous novelist. Yeats had come all the way from Dublin
and was strolling by the local butcher shop on his way to
the weird ceremony. (Moore was cremated and his ashes scattered
on an island near his home.) The village postman, cycling past,
yelled to the butcher: "Well, old Moore is dead at last!"

"Yes," said the butcher, "so I hear. What complaint?"

"Who's complaining?" asked the postman and blithely pedalled
away.

Was George Moore happy? I very much doubt it, if one can

judge by the underlying neuroticism in his novels. One of George Moore's contemporaries, Arnold Bennett, insisted that the most important lesson he learned from life was that he who makes happiness his chief objective in life is bound to fail. For, he insisted, happiness is a by-product, not an end in itself.

Arnold Bennett left his wife and ran off with an actress whom he was unable to marry. How well I recall meeting *the* Mrs. Arnold Bennett at a luncheon party in London many years ago. I was seated next to a very odd-looking woman wearing a crimson hat and dressed in a fashion of a former generation. I asked her name and she said:

"I am Mrs. Arnold Bennett, the wife of the famous writer. My husband is living in sin with another woman and I dress like this because I want everyone to ask who I am. In that way the world will eventually know that there is a Mrs. Arnold Bennett!"

Another Englishman-of-letters who bequeathed to the public domain an anecdotal heritage, was Sir Arthur Conan Doyle. Despite his macabre interest in communication with the dead, he was always full of fun. He spent considerable money and even sacrificed his reputation to some extent in order to promote his spiritualistic beliefs. At a meeting where he was expounding his views on the subject, a number of reporters were seated almost under his lectern.

With a wave of the hand, Sir Arthur knocked over a glass of water, spilling it over the gentlemen of the press.

"So sorry!" he said, his eyes twinkling, "I seem to have baptized you, even if I don't succeed in converting you."

While his beliefs were always under attack, his sincerity was never questioned. At a dinner party given in his honor by a New York society hostess, Doyle was telling of the joys to be derived from Spiritualism. But his hostess did everything to get him off the topic.

"I assure you, Sir Arthur," she said, "I believe in the immortality of the soul and all that sort of thing. But can we not talk of something more cheerful?"

Once Sir Arthur arrived in Paris from the South of France and after reaching his hotel by taxi, he paid the fare and the driver said in perfect English:

"You are Sir Arthur Conan Doyle, aren't you?"

The father of Sherlock Holmes was startled. "Yes," he said, "I am Conan Doyle, but how did you know?"

"Well, you see," said the driver mysteriously, "I am a Russian refugee and once worked in the Czar's Secret Service."

"Yes," said Doyle, "but that still does not tell me how you knew me."

"Oh, we learned all sorts of ways of detecting identity when I was in the Czar's service, sir."

"For instance?"

"Well, the name on your luggage helped me, and then there was a good photograph of you in the newspaper last evening!"

Every writer has his own theory of what particular conditions produce his best work. Balzac insisted that in order to produce a good book it was necessary for him to be chaste. So whenever he had an affair with a woman he whispered to himself: "There goes another masterpiece!"

Balzac, by the way, always wrote at night until sunrise. He once boasted that he possessed the Napoleonic "three o'clock courage," because he completed one of his novels at 3 A.M., and instead of going to bed and celebrating the next day, as most authors would have done, he took another sheet of paper and began the outline for a new book.

Once Flaubert, who began life as a physician, asked Balzac to criticize a book manuscript. In his report Balzac said: "You love to diagnose and prescribe for your characters who are obviously your patients. And like every good physician you end in putting all of them to death."

Ruskin once told off an impertinent critic with similar invective. The man had written a piece on the great English writer, who was always fulminating against the unaesthetic effects of the Industrial Revolution in England. The critic pointed out that Ruskin owed the Revolution a debt for the modern methods used in printing his books. Ruskin wrote to him:

"My meaning has always been that hearts should not be made of iron, nor heads of wood—and this last statement you may wisely consider when next it enters into your thick head to write about my views."

Recently I picked up two delightful literary curiosities about André Gide. On his country estate he kept chickens and amused himself by calling them after some of his friends. One coy-looking bird he called after his friend Colette, the famous novelist.

One day Colette came to see Gide and asked how her namesake was doing.

"I have some bad news for you," said Gide. "We have found out that Colette is actually Paul Valery!"

In his younger days André Gide spent much time in Paris where a maiden aunt kept house for him. A weekly event in the house was a breakfast which assembled at his home men of leading rank in literature. In addition, there came to the breakfasts people of second rank and some of unsavory reputation about whom Mademoiselle Gide did not hesitate to express her disdain.

At one of these affairs there was a discussion as to whether a noted murderer, scheduled to be guillotined, had been put to death or not. Mademoiselle Gide intervened: "Oh," she said with an ironic frown, "you may be sure that he has been guillotined or he would be present this morning."

Gide lost no love for women in his life; in fact, the dislike he had for some of them continued even after they died. When asked by a friend to compose an epitaph for a famous actress, who —unbeknown to the friend—Gide secretly hated, the first thing that came to mind was: "Asleep alone at last."

An English writer who had no use for monastic seclusion was H. G. Wells, who had mistresses galore (sometimes three or four at the same time!). He carried on his thinking and writing usually in the country where he could embrace his other mistress, Nature, as well. He once said that at fifty a man is either a gardener or a drunkard; and when one of his mistresses asked if she could publish his love letters to her, he consented on a fifty percent arrangement.

Anyhow, the author of *The Invisible Man* could tell some very tall tales privately, as can be imagined. Once, during a trip he took to Florida, he and a party of friends were motoring near Sarasota. The auto, in which they were driving, skidded and went off the road into a culvert. No one was hurt, but the car was temporarily incapacitated. Wells climbed out of the car and flagged a passing motorist. Out of the car stepped a man who gazed sympathetically at the mishap.

"We'll need an elephant to get us out of this," sighed H. G. Wells.

The man shook with laughter. "Wait here," he said. "I'll be right back."

Sure enough, in about half an hour, there came lumbering along the road the same man on the back of an elephant. It turned out that he was one of the circus trainers wintering nearby. According to Wells, the car was rescued through the intercession of elephant and trainer, and the party continued their drive.

The best elephant story used to be told by Robert Benchley, about the circus performing in an Icelandic village. A small elephant escaped into the surrounding environs of the district. Next day a woman inhabitant, who had never seen an elephant before, came running to the house of the Mayor, shouting excitedly: "There's the most unusual animal in my back yard. He's got the biggest tail I've ever seen. And he's pulling up cabbages with it . . ."

"Cabbages?" asked the Mayor, knowing that a vegetable is a

precious commodity in Iceland. "What's he doing with them?"

"I'd rather not say," answered the woman, blushing.

Returning, however, to literary vituperation, there was once a Poet Laureate of nineteenth century England named Alfred Austin, whose poetic merit was a matter of debate. Most thought his poetry worthless, but because he had an official position, he was highly touted by a few undiscriminating critics. To add to the controversy, Austin was a vain and pompous man.

Many people felt that Kipling ought to have the position of Poet Laureate in Austin's stead, but he had been ruled out because of a rude poem he had written about Queen Victoria called *The Widow of Windsor*. One day a Kipling protagonist, named Lord Young, met Alfred Austin and jocosely asked him if he would be able to make a living with his poetry, had he not private means of his own.

"I manage to keep the wolf from the door," said Austin smartly.

"How—by reading your poems to him?" Lord Young retorted.

Wordsworth was also a very conceited man. A vast portion of his verse is unreadable, but a small amount of it is very beautiful. Speaking to Charles Lamb he said: "I believe I could write like Shakespeare, if I had the mind to try." And Lamb's reply came as fast as his stutter would allow: "Yes, n-nothing would be w-wanting but the m-mind!"

Even as a boy Lamb had a superlative wit. His father took him into a cemetery to lay a wreath on the grave of his mother. As Charles passed down the long avenues of graves, he read a few of the eulogistic inscriptions on the headstones.

"Please tell me, Daddy," he asked, wonderstruck, "where do they bury all the naughty people?"

By far the best book ever written about gravestones is *Old Mortality* by Sir Walter Scott, whose leading character, Robert Paterson, clandestinely kept the graves of the Covenanters in good order.

Scott was a kindly man but, when necessary, could turn on another side of himself. Once, during a conversation with Coleridge and Wordsworth, the latter made a sweeping statement about philosophers.

"I have the greatest contempt for Aristotle," he said.

Scott glared at him fiercely: "But not, I take it, that contempt which familiarity breeds."

Book-borrowers were the bane of Scott's existence. He once said: "Most of my friends are good book-keepers."

And another time he declared that his main reason for visiting certain friends was for the purpose of looking over his own library.

At a dinner party given in his honor by Lady Blessington, a very frivolous society beauty, his hostess professed to be a great admirer of his work and insisted that books authored by Scott were her best friends.

Later she took Scott to her library and directed his attention to a set of his Waverly novels. Noticing that the edition was an early one, he reached for it and pulled out one of the volumes.

Perusing it with reverent care, he found the pages uncut.

"I understand now, my dear Lady Blessington, why you call my books your friends. You do not cut them!"

To show how irritating these kinds of admirers can be, there is an instance in the life of Noah Webster, the great American lexicographer, who spent almost his whole existence compiling the dictionary which today bears his name. He was a dour sort of man and intrinsically disliked society. However, at a literary affair which he was forced to attend, a "bluestocking" type of woman said to him: "Mr. Webster, I was disgusted to find a very obscene word in your dictionary. My admiration for you is waning . . ."

"Now, now!" said Webster. "You wouldn't have known the word was there if you hadn't looked it up!"

Noah Webster was a grammarian in the strictest sense and

when asked to pass on the prose of a famous writer of the day, snorted: "He wrote excellent English until he discovered grammar."

Which might be said of many writers of this year of grace. George Ade, a writer of American slang, was once asked by a German publisher if his latest book had been translated into that language.

"Heavens!" said Ade. "It's not even yet translated into English!"

... 2

Hollywood Hilarity

Many world-famous persons have flashed their satire at Hollywood. Jean Couteau described it as "an insane asylum run by its own inmates." And it was stigmatized by Maurice Maeterlinck as "a cultural desert." Ferenc Molnar called it "a sunny place for shady people," and J. B. Priestley declared that as a civic institution it was "a series of suburbs in search of a city." If I may be allowed to quote from myself, I once said: "Hollywood is not uncivilized. It is decivilized."

Am I wrong in thinking that in becoming more dynamic since movies were taught to talk, Hollywood has lost something of itself? There was something more glamorous about the silent, shadowy days, with the inevitable scenes of kissing and tears, renunciation in a drawing room and reconciliation in a taxi—the escape for the masses from picturesque poverty to picturesque plenty. Is this a sign of age on my part? Am I merely yearning for the halcyon days of the Twenties?

What joy Pearl White brought to her audiences, who weekly devoured the new chapter in her endless serials! In making these perilous films, this actress underwent many ordeals, giving the portmanteau title to her "cliff-hangers," *The Perils of Pauline.*

In one of these early successes Miss White was to be filmed

jumping over a precipitous declivity, at the bottom of which was a large pool of water.

Carefully Pearl waded into the pool and found it rather shallow. Anxiously she spoke to her director, a man fond of pulling her leg. "There's only one foot of water over there," she exclaimed, waving her hand in the direction of the set.

"I know, Pearl," countered the director. "Do you think we want you to drown?"

A little later on, it became the fashion for Hollywood producers to raid good literature with rather unhappy results. Thus, that fine play, *The Admirable Crichton* by Sir James Barrie (which is about a family butler who bosses his master when they are wrecked on a desert island), was made into a film entitled *Male and Female*. The change in title was made, if you please, because it was feared that the public might be misled into thinking that the story had a naval theme!

Mere titles were bought from time to time from certain lucky authors. A book of sexual philosophy was purchased for a large sum from Havelock Ellis, the renowned sexologist, entitled *The Dance of Life*. Nothing was used but the title, doubtless because it was thought that the name of Havelock Ellis, associated as it was with sexology, would help box office receipts.

All this was very nice literary marketing, if you could get it. At the same time, can one wonder why Samuel Goldwyn said, perhaps despairing of Hollywood moronia: "I want to go where the hand of man has never set foot."

Finally even he succumbed to the new craze to make the movies into an art form. He imported two world-famous writers, Maurice Maeterlinck and later Ferenc Molnar.

When Maeterlinck arrived by train in Los Angeles, Goldwyn himself met the great Belgian poet at the station. Greeting him and his young wife, Goldwyn said: "You are such a great writer that I would hesitate to tell you what to write about. Why not take what you think is your best work and turn it into a scenario?"

So Maeterlinck, who had written about many subjects, including blue birds and bees, retired to an ivory tower for several months, working on his film assignment at fifteen hundred dollars a week.

Upon completion of the script, he handed the bulky thing to Goldwyn, who took it, thumbed through a few pages, and uttered a cry. Tearing what little hair he had left, he exclaimed: "My God, the hero is a bee!" Incidentally, nothing Maeterlinck wrote during his Hollywood stint of writing was ever filmed.

A story told about Molnar is probably just as apocryphal, and concerns his first film assignment. The movie mogul, whose charge he was, put him in an office adjoining his at the studio. An aperture in the door enabled the official to keep an eye on what the highly-paid Molnar was doing with his time. Regularly an office boy peeped through and made a report.

The first of these reports alarmed the official. "Mr. Molnar is surrounded by open books on his desk," said the office boy, "but he does nothing but stare at the ceiling."

The movie mogul went himself and looked through the aperture only to have the report confirmed. Days passed and Molnar was observed in the same pose—sitting back in his chair and staring blankly at the ceiling.

Finally the official obtained the services of an interpreter, since Molnar did not speak much English at the time, and together they went to the writer's office. "Ask Mr. Molnar why he is continually staring at the ceiling," ordered the official.

Molnar cleared his throat in anticipation of lengthy argument. "I stare at the ceiling because I am thinking," he said coolly.

"Tell Mr. Molnar not to *think*," ordered the official to the interpreter. "Tell him to *write*."

And not much thinking of a profound type was done in the days of Theda Bara (whose real name was Theodosia Goodman) and that era of Hollywood hokum. She was called an Arabian actress because it was said at that time all other races were represented on the silver sheet. So her screen name was manufactured by spelling Arab backwards and she was presented to the gullible American public as "the greatest living actress, alive or dead!"

Soon Miss Bara became more celebrated for exposing as much of her person as her publicity agents dared, and she was dubbed by her detractors as Theda "Barer." In due course of time she wished to try her talent in a great dramatic part. It was decided by her studio to cast her in the taxing role of Thaïs, in the story of that name by Anatole France.

At the script reading prior to production of the film, Miss Bara sat transfixed by the moving saga. A typical gentleman of the film world, recently graduated from the cloak and suit trade, was reading the script. Not being familiar with the subtleties of French pronunciation, he could only say "Thighs" when referring to the heroine. So he went bravely on, reading how the hero held "Thighs," pressed "Thighs" to him and kissed "Thighs" passionately.

The reading had not gone far, when Miss Bara held up her hand. With a fierce glance of her sultry eyes at the group, she said: "I'm not going to have all that done to my thighs. Give the part to someone who likes that sort of thing." And she sailed out in high dudgeon. The part was eventually awarded to the singer, Mary Garden.

All the same, Theda Bara represented an epoch of the film industry, and her fan mail glutted the Hollywood postal service. Once she received a letter from a Chinaman in Peking. He wrote: "Honorable Theda Bara. Please send me your honorable picture, as honorably soon as possible and as honorably naked as possible."

Of the same epoch as Theda Bara was Carl Laemmle, an avuncular figure without whom Hollywood might not be the booming town it is today. "Uncle" Carl, as he was known affectionately to his friends, was one of the pioneers who helped to create the multi-billion-dollar film industry of California.

If this pleasant man lacked the polish of a formal education, he knew how to turn out moving pictures which the public liked. He was never afraid to gamble, and he possessed commercial imagination. And so it was one day that he announced to his secretary that he had purchased a French novel called *The Prisoner*. This book happened to be one of those which was considered salacious thirty years ago, but today would probably send the average sensation seeker to sleep.

"Uncle" Carl's secretary had read the book and was horrified. "Mr. Laemmle!" she exclaimed. "You never can make a movie of that story. It's about two lesbians."

"Oh, hell," said "Uncle" Carl, shrugging his huge shoulders, "what's the difference? We'll call them two Italians."

Masters of this sort of error in connotation abound in Hollywood down to the present hour. The chief exponent used to be Samuel Goldwyn, who once told a sculptor who expressed admiration of Mrs. Goldwyn's beautiful hands to "make a bust of them."

Now Michael Curtiz, a top-ranking director, rules supreme in this field. He is on record as having uttered the following "Goldwynisms." During the making of a large film spectacle, he ordered the extras in one of the scenes to "separate together in a bunch." To Gary Cooper whom he was directing in a solo scene with the star on horseback, he said: "Now ride off in all directions." And another time when an assistant tried to explain something about the script which they were filming, he fired: "Don't talk to me while I am interrupting."

All directors are not so charmingly amusing, and some resort to sarcasm and invective. During the filming of *The Razor's Edge* (after the novel by Somerset Maugham), Tyrone Power seemed to be having difficulty grasping the symbolism underlying his role. As readers of the novel will recall, it was about a young man who sets out on a search for truth and is finally cut by it, as with the edge of a razor. In desperation, Darryl Zanuck is supposed to have said to Power: "Do I have to bring my barber here for technical director?"

Zanuck is a good example of what Hollywood opportunism and promotional ability can do. He exhales bluster and baloney in just the right proportions. When Hugh Walpole, the famous British novelist, was in Hollywood writing scenarios or turning some of his novels into films, Zanuck asked him to see some "rushes" of a film he had just produced. Walpole accepted for diplomatic reasons, but secretly he disliked the average Hollywood product.

In the midst of the most poignant part of the picture, Walpole was seized by a violent attack of hay fever. He did his best to stifle his sneezes and he was very relieved when the "rushes" were finished. They were very mawkish scenes and badly acted, but Zanuck was profoundly moved by them. As soon as the lights went up, he looked at Walpole whose eyes were wet with tears from sneezing. Patting him on the shoulder, he said: "No need to be ashamed. I was just as affected. But somehow I never cry."

Walpole wrote several successful films and even played small parts in a few of them. Wherever he went, he carried his tea-making equipment along. One of the studio hands asked him one day: "How many cups of tea does it take you to write a book?"

Walpole scratched his head. "Oh, I should say these days I write about five hundred words to the cup."

Harking back to the early days of Hollywood, Cecil B. De Mille is a man who can regale his friends with a lot of good stories when he is in the mood. During his first directing years he battled as best he could against the ignorance which was then in power. Once when making a great religious spectacle, Mr. De Mille's producer was a man who exercised his privilege by dumbfounding everybody with exhibitions of his stupidity.

One morning, it is said, the man came on the set to see how things were shaping up in the production. "Tell me," he said to

De Mille, "where are those men I saw yesterday dressed in night shirts? They don't seem to be in evidence today."

De Mille could hardly stifle a laugh. "Why, they are the Twelve Apostles. I'm not using them today."

"Well," continued the producer, "they looked pretty effective. You know I never stint expense. Put in a dozen more of them."

What a debt the American public owes to Cecil B. De Mille, whose artistic integrity is manifested in all his work. A man usually courteous and kind, he can also turn on another side when necessary.

Recently, the story goes, a Hollywood artists' representative was trying to sell him some talent which had seen its best days. The agent insisted that the actors and actresses whom he represented were not too old for the parts available in *The Ten Commandments*. Finally De Mille exclaimed: "I know I am doing a biblical film, but I am *not* going to use the original cast!"

Incidentally, when the first version of *The Ten Commandments* appeared, way back during the silent era, Will Rogers commented: "*The Ten Commandments* is a fine film up to the point where God finishes and the script writer takes over."

Hollywood actors enjoy star billing on book jackets as well as marquees, and so there have been those who have taken to the typewriter. Frequently, of course, "ghosts" cast their shadows on these literary endeavors. Errol Flynn insists that the novel which bears his name is, in fact, his own—and, judging by the reviews, one cannot but believe him.

But there was the case of another film star, who shall be nameless, who, for reasons of vanity, became an author. Those of his own circle knew that he had not written the book himself, for he spent all his time (and still does in between pictures) doing the rounds of bars and cafés.

One day the star met a Hollywood script writer who was well aware of the prevarication. A new book by the star had just appeared. "Have you read my latest book?" he asked rather patronizingly.

The script writer chuckled fiendishly and said: "No! Have you?"

Of course, no one would blame a film star for wishing to become an author. Such an ambition is praiseworthy indeed, and should be encouraged in order to combat the Hollywood trend towards nihilism.

Albert Einstein spent a short time in Hollywood many years ago. When asked by a friend to analyze the atmosphere there, he wrinkled his fine brow and said: "Can a fish describe the murky water in which he swims?"

The patron saint of relativity was introduced to Charlie Chaplin, whose avidity for erudition has never decreased. On an outing together they were driving along Hollywood Boulevard in an open car. Quickly a few of the alert passers-by noticed them and began cheering: "Hurrah for Charlie! Hurrah for Charlie!"

Modestly, Charlie pointed to Einstein who had been well publicized in the newspapers, and the crowd began: "Hurrah for Einstein! Hurrah for Einstein! Hurrah for Charlie!"

An innately humble man, Einstein could not understand why the cheering crowd should be so interested in him, putting it all down to Chaplin's popularity.

"You see," explained Chaplin, "they are cheering me because they understand me and you because they don't."

Infused with what Kipling called "'satiable curiosity," Chaplin read Einstein's books avidly and once loaned one of them to Ernest Lubitsch. Later he asked the famous director how he had liked it:

"Very much," said Lubitsch with an engaging smile. "That fellow Einstein has a lot of my ideas."

Einstein's theory of time should please the average actress who tries to take a few years off her own age and add it on to that of another woman.

One automatically thinks of one of Beatrice Lillie's famous sarcasms. A certain film star, known for her age prevarication, said to Bea at a party: "How I hate to think of life at forty-five!"

"And what happened then?" asked Bea, showing her fangs.

In private life Bea Lillie is Lady Peel, and the story goes that she telephoned to Mary Pickford who was then learning French: "C'est Lady Parle qui Peel!"

In any case, how can one blame a woman for lying about her age? For instance, does an actress like Joan Crawford have an age at all? And who would think that she is slowly crossing the bridge which leads to middle age? Like many a film star, she has a good library and is one of the few actresses who reads the classics. The story is told about a celebrated writer whom she was once entertaining and who complimented her on her taste in books.

"You see," said Joan, flattered, "my mother always gives me a book on my birthdays!"

Here her husband broke in: "You can also see," he said, grinning broadly, "that Joan has a pretty large library!"

Actually the Cinderella story of the girl without anything, who works hard and ends up with everything, sums itself up in Joan Crawford. She may not have had the advantages of a formal education, but she has plenty of absorptive power and has always been alert to opportunities for self-improvement.

In between marriages Joan was on a visit to England and was spending an evening with a titled Englishman, whom she wanted to impress. She had read books and books on English customs, and one thing had stuck in her mind—that Yorkshire pudding was a speciality of English cuisine.

However, at that time Hollywood did not possess restaurants which make a fad of foreign foods such as English Roast Beef, which is now associated in the American mind with Yorkshire pudding.

Anyway, at the end of a good dinner, just at the point when the Englishman was saying to himself that Hollywood film stars were much maligned people and *did* possess culture, Joan ruined everything. The gentleman asked: "What will you have for dessert, my dear?"

"I think I'll have some Yorkshire pudding," said Joan, as she smiled bewitchingly.

The first time that Bette Davis went to London she received a shock from which she took time to recover. On this particular trip the famous star became legally embattled over whether she had the right to make a film for a British company or was bound solely to her Hollywood studio. So Bette obtained the best counsel available, one Lord Jowett who is known behind his back by his colleagues as "Stuffy." He is a man who exudes the old-world reserve of a Dickensian character.

Bette went for her first interview with him in his chambers, which happen to be situated just off the Strand in the Inner Temple. It so happened that a picture starring Bette Davis was playing at a cinema nearby, with her name in bright lights shining up and down the Strand.

During the opening commonplaces of conversation between Lord Jowett and Miss Davis, one of his first questions was, "May I ask your occupation?"

Slightly crestfallen, Bette swallowed her pride and answered meekly: "I act in the movies. As a matter of fact one of my pictures is playing across the street. You can actually see my name on the marquee from this window."

Lord Jowett eyed her biliously: "I know there's some form of entertainment across the street, but I wasn't sure exactly what it was."

As a matter of fact, Bette Davis is one of the few actresses who has never become topsy-turvy over her success. Some stars who have been catapulted into the stellar constellations are apt to have their feet planted firmly in mid-air. And then there are those to whom the demands of fame are anathema. Such an one is Greta

Garbo. However, even in her heyday, Greta was not in every land the success she was in the U.S.A. In Ireland, for instance, her films were never as popular as those of Bette Davis. Whenever one of Garbo's pictures came to Dublin, the Irish stayed away in thousands, which led a critic to remark apropos of Greta's overwhelming desire for solitude: "If Greta really wants to be alone, she should come to a performance of one of her films in Dublin."

Which sounds like one of Hedda Hopper's acid remarks. Hedda has chalked up to her credit many a witticism. Did she not create the famous phrase: "No actress is better than her last picture"?

Results are certainly the main thing which count in Hollywood. Everyone is after a good job and will not stop at double-crossing his friends to obtain it. When a delegation of producers went abroad after the war to inspect film facilities in various European countries, someone asked Hedda Hopper how they could afford to absent themselves so long and find their jobs awaiting them upon their return.

"Perhaps," replied Hedda, "they are relying on their anti-tetanus injections to keep them immune from the old knife-in-the-back."

Studio officials sometimes fool themselves, as for instance in the incipient stage of Rudolph Valentino's career. None of them could foresee the immortality to which this amazing personality was to be heir. The story goes that his wife, an executive young woman named Natascha Rambova, went to see one of the studio heads about a raise in his salary. The official is said to have replied: "Please remember that this studio has spent over one hundred thousand dollars trying to fool the American public about your husband. Now don't you get fooled, too."

Now and again a star poses a little too much for his own good. Henry Fonda became so Lincolnesque in his manner after making *Abe Lincoln in Illinois* that even his countenance wore the rustic aura and the sadness so noticeable on the face of the Great Liberator.

Leo McCarey, a director with a "tongue," is credited with the observation: "Fonda still thinks he's Lincoln and can't wait for the assassination."

No one could ever accuse Eddie Cantor of posing, yet he was once taken down very neatly by a child. He was appearing in a vaudeville act at a theater in Wichita, Kansas, and, when he left the stage door after his appearance, was approached by several small boys for an autograph.

Willingly he signed for the children and when he had finished he noticed a smaller boy lurking shyly in a corner.

"How do you do," said Eddie. "Don't you want my autograph, also?"

The boy put his hands in his pockets, walked in the other direction and threw a fierce look over his shoulder: "Hell, no!" he said. "I was waiting for you to get through with your act so I can see *Donald Duck.*"

Alec Guiness had an amusing experience in London. He was walking along Oxford Street and a passer-by stopped in his tracks, and stared point-blank at the great actor. Guiness gave the man the sort of smile appropriate for an admirer. And then the man sidled up to him.

"I know I've seen your picture somewhere," he said.

"Yes," said Guiness, "you probably have."

"It was only the other day," continued the man.

"No doubt you were reading about me in the *Telegraph?*"

"I know where it was," said the man, as if struck by a great revelation. "It was an advertisement for Doane's Pills. What was it again you were cured of?"

Misapprehensions occur even in the social life of Hollywood. When Florence Vidor married the great violinist Jascha Heifetz, no one paid much attention. One evening a few of her friends decided to give her a party to celebrate her marriage. Proffering the invitation by telephone, the spokesman said: "I believe your hubby plays the fiddle. Tell him to bring it along and give us a tune."

The fact is that visiting celebrities are received in Hollywood "calmly and with a touch of lethargy," as some wit has said. When a star marries a title, the impact may be harder. We heard such references as "royal romance" applied in the newspapers to the marriages of Rita Hayworth and Grace Kelly in connection with their respective princes.

Of course, Rainier of Monaco is not a Royal Highness, but a Serene Highness; and while he holds the hereditary rank of an old dynasty he is, by the way, descended from pirates!

Many of the brightest epigrams have been made by Joan Fontaine, known locally as "the wit of the movies." One day she visited the same set as the one where Orson Welles was making a picture. Welles was in the midst of doing a scene in which he was about to be burned to death in bed. The director was demanding the usual repeat "takes" which was making Welles nervous despite the fireproofing precautions which had been taken.

With the flames crackling around his enormous bulk, Welles yelled to Joan from his funeral pyre: "Gad, I'll be glad when this is over. I now know what Joan of Arc endured!"

"Keep your spirits up," quipped Joan Fontaine. "We'll let you know if we get the odor of burning ham."

Another time, before Joan became a star of magnitude, she was being "upstaged" by a famous actress who was at that period of her career known as the "nose-dive." In the picture Joan was playing a featured part and with the charm that is all her own, she let the star know how she felt about her rude methods.

"Just remember, Miss Fontaine, that I am a star," the actress replied haughtily.

"And don't you wish you were a meteor?" was Joan's rejoinder.

All stars who have been on the billboards since they were young are apt to be spoken of as museum exhibits. In Ireland there is a delightful saying: "I don't know how old you are, but you don't look it."

Gloria Swanson is an actress who is truly ageless. However, she tells the story about the time when she was acting near New York in a play. A knock came at her dressing room door after the performance and Miss Swanson beheld a group of ladies all in their sixties. They obviously belonged to a theater party.

"Miss Swanson," the spokesman began, "we felt we had to come and say hello because we all remember you when we were girls!"

On that particular evening Miss Swanson was tired and irritable.

"That's a damned lie," she said. "You're all ten years older than me. Now off with you!"

Dorothy McKail, one-time bright star of the silent films, had a similar experience. She was recently traveling on a transcontinental train to California and, during one of the station-stops, she was pacing the platform. An elderly, gray-haired woman addressed her quizzically: "By any chance are you Dorothy McKail?"

One should hasten to add that anyone who remembers Miss McKail in the silent films would readily recognize her loveliness today. Miss McKail nodded. A little breathlessly the woman continued: "Do you remember a film you made years ago, named *From Heaven Sent*?"

Miss McKail nodded again and the woman became more excited.

"Do you recall a scene in that film where you held a baby at a christening?"

Miss McKail answered affirmatively with an engaging smile.

"Well," the woman said in a slow measured tone as if she were about to divulge a great secret, "I'm the baby!"

There was a time when the position of a film star could be undermined in the public eye by having a baby, no matter how heavily married she may have been. And so the birth of a son to one of the stars of silent film days put Carl Laemmle, who owned her contract, into a "tizzie."

Calling upon her at the hospital he went through the necessary formalities of congratulations, but his manner betrayed his anxiety over the star's future.

"Don't look so glum, 'Unc,'" she said, hugging the baby to her breast, "this is my finest production!"

"Yes," said "Uncle" Carl, "perhaps you are right. But how can I title and release it?"

... 3

Dramatic Drollery

Some of the best epigrams about theatrical life come from dramatic critics. Who was it who stigmatized Broadway openings as having a "first-knife" audience? Possibly Alexander Woollcott, a critic who did some knifing himself. Of John Barrymore he said: "There's nothing wrong with Jack that a miracle can't cure." And about a play called *The Lake,* starring Katharine Hepburn, he commented: "If this play lasts overnight it should not only be considered a long run, but a revival as well."

George Jean Nathan is a critic who is famous for withering remarks about plays he does not like. He called *The Righteous Are Bold,* a recent Broadway offering which flopped overnight, "A cheap marked-down bargain basement type of play," and suggested that the management would be better off relying on the sale of orangeade rather than tickets—so "papered" was the house.

When Walter Winchell was barred on first night openings from all the Schubert theaters because of his scurrilous criticisms, he said he would go to their closings by waiting a few days. Was it Walter Winchell who said about *The Hero in Man* that most of the heroes were in the audience? And who were the critics who roundly insulted each other? One said: "You are a good reason for birth control!"

And the other said: "You are a eunuch. You know all about it and can't do it!"

Gone are the days when we had brilliant critics like Eugene Field to regale us. Reviewing the performance of Sir Johnston Forbes Robertson in *Richard II*, the famous poet wrote: "He plays the King as if he were about to play the ace."

And of a poor performance of *Uncle Tom's Cabin* he wrote simply: "The Irish wolfhound was very poorly supported by the cast."

And of a very spectacular musical, the same critic exclaimed: "I wouldn't leave a turn unstoned."

Speaking of Katharine Hepburn in *The Lake*, which played on Broadway a very long time ago, this film star was then supported by a fine American actress named Blanche Bates. At this particular time Miss Hepburn was not as at home on the stage as she may be now, and she also suffered badly from "nerves."

So in order to keep her mind riveted upon her lines she had constructed for her use a passage made of screens which led from her dressing room door to the wings of the stage. The imagination boggles in wondering what epithets were hurled by the stage hands because of this!

At a performance of the play, Dorothy Parker, famed for her adept verbal slashings, went backstage to see her friend Blanche Bates. Miss Parker had been told about the screen passage and when asked by one of the friends accompanying her about it, she said dryly: "That's to prevent Katharine Hepburn from catching acting off Blanche Bates."

Film stars do not usually have the struggle which confronts great stage actresses. Some of the finest dramatic actresses have had difficulties breaking into their careers, and one can safely say they are all the better for it. To quote from the Bible, "many are called and few are chosen." In the legitimate theater there must be a thousand failures for every success. Katina Paxinou, the Greek tragic actress, encountered the usual opposition at first. But being a woman with an original mind, she hit on a clever ruse to obtain her first important role.

A London producer was shortly going to stage a production of Ibsen's *Ghosts* and Madame Paxinou heard that he had his mind set on an actress of note, which made her all the more anxious to obtain the part of Mrs. Alving.

First she called upon the producer at his offices, dressed fashionably and looking enchantingly beautiful. This made little impression on the man since he felt that the role should be played by an actress who possessed a soured and embittered mien. He explained his views in so many words and brought the interview to a close.

However, Madame Paxinou's surpassing charm made an impression upon him from the social point of view, and she managed to prevail upon the producer to call and see her the following evening.

In answer to the ring at her door, the man was confronted by a hard-faced woman with hair tightly brushed back and done up in a bun behind. Taking her to be the charwoman, he said: "I have an appointment with Madame Paxinou."

The formidable-looking woman frowned in a most unfriendly way. Then sternly she said: "I am Madame Paxinou!"

The producer stammered, for he found it impossible to believe that this was the same woman he had met earlier in the day. Still frowning, she said: "I am Madame Paxinou as Mme. Alving! And now do I get the part?" (She did.)

This gift of so identifying themselves with their roles is undoubtedly the stamp of greatness. However, it results in their not always finding it easy to shift back into their own personalities. I recall dining with George Arliss after he had been playing the part of Disraeli. Evidently the transition had not taken place, for I found myself saying to him: "It is hard to believe I am talking to George Arliss!"

"You're not," he snapped in that terse manner of his. "I am still Benjamin Disraeli."

The same phenomenon applies to playwrights. They have to live with their characters mentally in order to bring them to life. Once during a conversation with Maurice Maeterlinck I referred to his famous play *Monna Vanna* which is set in the period of the Renaissance.

In the story the Conqueror of Pisa makes it one of his peace conditions that the Governor's daughter present herself to him at his camp naked under her mantle.

Monna Vanna agrees to give herself in this way to the Conqueror. But, I argued with Maeterlinck, I did not think it likely that the father of the young woman would allow her to present herself in the attire specified. Monna Vanna, I agreed, would be willing to exhange her virtue for the safety of her city, but would she go to him gowned only in her mantle?

Maeterlinck assumed his favorite attitude, elbows on his knees and fingers gently touching.

"There you are quite wrong," he said, irritated. "Because I *saw* her do it!"

And then he went on to tell me of the method he used in creating his characters. In his mind they soon became more living than the living—and he would await the inevitable clash of character upon character. They would thus write the play for him!

In the days of the revival of Irish literature and art, it was indeed a happy fortune which brought together such a group of talented playwrights and players who could do such excellent justice to the cause. Witness, for instance, how the Irish playwrights of that period dramatized their grievance against England so that the whole world got to know about it—a great literary achievement.

The entire movement sums itself up in Lady Gregory and William Butler Yeats, two great personalities with a profound sense of theater. A story is told about a time they were auditioning some new talent and an aspiring actor named Barry Fitzgerald came before them.

Mr. Fitzgerald had chosen for the purpose of showing off his ability a piece from Shakespeare. When he uttered the inevitable "O, what a rogue and peasant slave am I . . ." he encountered difficulty.

"Ach," he sighed, "I think I'll do it better without me teeth."

And with that he emptied his gums and finished the scene.

Needless to say, Lady Gregory and Yeats were bursting with laughter.

"You are a comedian and should never play tragedy," said Yeats when he got control of himself.

"Yes," said Lady Gregory, still chuckling, "you will play a roistering parson in our next Abbey Theater production."

Thus a great career was born, almost by accident, and we have to thank the vision of Yeats and Lady Gregory.

But one should not be led to believe that this sort of thing happens often. Without a thorough knowledge of tragedy, Barry Fitzgerald could not play comedy. And most auditions are not nearly so happy, as the following proves.

Yeats was listening on another occasion to an aspiring Thespian, a young man of the long hair and flowing tie variety. Yeats listened, rather agonized, as the young man evidenced all the stigmata of effeminacy. It was easy to see that the chances of his ever becoming an actor were exceedingly slight.

"Would you please go back a little farther?" requested Yeats. "You are standing too near to the footlights."

The young man took a step backwards and continued doing violence to a scene by Synge. Yeats could stand no more.

"Go back a little farther, please," he said, with a note of sarcasm in his voice.

"But Mr. Yeats," said the young man, "if I go back any farther I shall be off the stage entirely."

"Exactly," said Mr. Yeats.

As a matter of fact, Yeats himself wore his hair a little long. He used to tell the story about his first excursion into playwrighting. It was a whimsical play called *The Land of Heart's Desire* which had its premiere performance in London.

Yeats was seated in the front row all alone on the opening night, and it was not long before he realized that the play was not pleasing the audience. As the curtain fell, a lady in the seat behind touched him on the shoulder and handed him something in an envelope.

"Someone told me that you are the author of this play."

"Correct, Madame," said Yeats.

"Well, my daughter collects souvenirs of great people, and I took the liberty of snipping a piece of your hair when you were concentrating on the play."

"You do take liberties, Madame," observed Yeats, touching the side of his head in a gesture of annoyance.

"That's the point, sir," the woman continued. "I now wish to give you back the piece of your hair I snipped."

"How so?"

"Well, I don't think it would fit into my daughter's collection."

It is, of course, well recognized, especially by members of the acting profession, that the manifestation of appreciation is essential to the exercise of their art. Max Reinhardt imposed stringent requirements upon his actors, but never did he fail to award praise when it was due.

He once directed Eleanora Duse in a play which he had written himself. The great Italian tragedienne was having her troubles with the German language, and it was especially painful to Reinhardt to hear his own lines misquoted. But the temperamental Duse hated to be placed in the wrong.

"I'll have you know that I know my lines, Mr. Reinhardt," she said indignantly.

"Yes," ejaculated Reinhardt, "perhaps you do. But you don't know mine."

Reinhardt owed his greatest fame to his impeccable production of *The Miracle,* a wordless play. Its success was considerably aided by the choice of Lady Diana Manners in the part of the Virgin. This beautiful Englishwoman was married to Duff Cooper, one-time Minister of War in the British Cabinet.

Inevitably mixing with stage society as well as diplomatic, she met Noel Coward. On the day they happened to meet, Lady Diana was in a bellicose frame of mind.

"Are *you* the Noel Coward who wrote a play called *Private Lives?*" she asked sarcastically.

Noel Coward answered that he was one and the same.

"Very funny," said Lady Diana, insinuatingly.

Noel Coward was momentarily taken aback, for he had tried to be pleasant.

"Tell me," he said, "could you be the Lady Diana Manners who played the Virgin in *The Miracle?*"

Of course the answer was in the affirmative.

"Very funny," sneered Coward and turned away.

As stated, the husband of Lady Diana Manners was Mr. Duff Cooper, who was never a friend to Ireland. Several times he had made unflattering remarks about Ireland in his official capacity. He finally retired from office because of ill-health and went on a cruise to regain his strength. But he failed to rally, and died aboard ship. One of the Dublin papers commented: "Mr. Duff Cooper has died where he always was—at sea."

This was cruel, but he had asked for it, just as his wife deserved the retort of Noel Coward, who can never be placed at a disadvantage. A master of the acid comment, he is a challenge to those who would win their spurs at this sort of sparring.

"Were you ever at Oxford or Cambridge, Mr. Coward?" asked a dinner companion intent on beating Coward at his own game.

The reply came with a thrust: "Oh, no. I was never at either. But my secretary went to Oxford, I believe."

All his friends know that underneath Noel Coward's seemingly caustic exterior is a heart of gold. He has even written plays for famous actresses who have seen their best days. And he has sometimes given the ladies a new lease on theatrical life.

Ingrates no doubt some of them have been, and the story is told that one day Noel was informed that one of them was running him down after all his kindness.

"Strange!" he said wryly. "I just can't understand it. She used to be my bosom friend. And now she's all bosom and no friend!"

This sort of treatment led Bernard Shaw to say of a so-called friend who acted the same way to him: "Funny, I don't remember doing him a good turn."

Most people will have forgotten, however, that Bernard Shaw owed his first success in the theater to Richard Mansfield. For years Shaw had been famous as a literary dramatist, with many published plays to his credit, but not until Mansfield produced *The Devil's Disciple* was he acclaimed.

This play made a fortune for both dramatist and actor-producer. But both paid a heavy price in dealing with the vagaries of each other. In one of Shaw's outbursts occasioned by disagreement with Mansfield, Shaw quipped:

"Kipling was absolutely right. East is East and West is West and never the twain shall meet!"

Later Mansfield said to a reporter: "I love *The Devil's Disciple*. I am the disciple all right. But why on earth did such a good play have to be written by Bernard Shaw?"

Of course Shaw had the last laugh. Theater-goers were familiar with Mansfield's background. He had mastered his craft the hard way, touring the major cities of America for years—and success in New York came later. Referring to the long training which the fine actor had obtained, he commented: "Poor Mansfield! He used to be a *force de tour*. Now, with the success of my play, he is a *tour de force!"*

Bernard Shaw and Sir Laurence Olivier crossed swords when the famous actor was acting the leading part in one of Shaw's many plays. He complained that the lines in a certain scene were too talkative and needed "re-write," as he had noticed members of the audience walking out at that point of the play.

"Young man," said Shaw, "you need never worry when you see people walking out of an audience. It is when they start rushing towards you that you should feel concerned!"

When Leslie Howard lost his life in enemy action during the last war, wide sympathy was expressed for his wife and children, but how many think of him now? Leslie did his early training in stock companies, one of which performed a different play every evening. During one of these performances he forgot his lines. In a hushed voice he whispered to the prompter: "Line, please?"

The prompter fumbled with a pile of scripts by his side.

"Line, hell! Which play is it?"

Audiences are unintentionally convulsed when an actor gets his signals crossed. John McCormack did some acting before he became a great singer. In Chicago he was playing in one of those agonizing types of melodramas. He was supposed to say to the villain, who was banging at the door: "If you put your head through that door, I'll put a bullet in it."

Instead, he twisted the line into: "If you put your bullet through that door, I'll put a head in it."

And Charles Kemble, the great English actor of a few generations ago, was once playing Hamlet and should have said: "Shall I lay perjury on my soul?"

Which he perverted into: "Shall I lay surgery on my poll?"

Maeterlinck told me about a painful, yet also humorous, experience when he went to see the premiere performance of his *Pelléas and Mélisande* performed in London. Mrs. Patrick Campbell was playing Mélisande in its legitimate stage version and, through a mistake in her lines, turned this poignant drama into a fiasco.

Those who do not know the play or opera must realize that the character of Mélisande is scarcely of this world and any injection of humor would be ruinous. And those who know the operatic version of this masterpiece will realize that the translator found considerable difficulty with the repetitious lament of "Je ne suis pas heureuse." Such a cadence is impossible to capture in the English language and all he could do was to render it as "I am not happy." Unfortunately this line is repeated several times.

When Mrs. Patrick Campbell came to the point where Mélisande finds herself unequal to face her husband, Golaud, who has caught his brother Pelléas making love to her, she is supposed to say: "I have not the courage!"

Instead Mrs. Campbell, to her horror, re-uttered the often-spoken line: "I am not happy!"

Only a playwright would know what this did to Maeterlinck who was stricken to the point of tears, while the audience burst into gales of laughter.

Among the many stories about Stella Campbell in London, there is the one told about an altercation she once had with a taxi driver. She was late in getting to the theater where she was acting at the time and was in a highly nervous state. Apparently her nerves reacted on the little Pekingese dog which she carried with her always, for he committed an indiscretion.

As she was paying her fare, the driver's eyes were directed to the floor of the cab where the dog was yapping proudly. The driver then looked at Mrs. Campbell indignantly, and cleared his throat for some diatribe.

"Don't you dare say a word," she countered, taking up the dog in her arms. "*I did it!*"

Poor Stella! She understood the gentle art of making enemies! Like Madame de Staël she would have said: "The more I see of men the more I love dogs!"

One of the kindest and best-loved women on the London stage was Gertrude Lawrence. At one time she had a dresser whose daughter had never seen Gertie on the stage. So she paid for a front-row seat at a matinee for the child to come and see her in her latest musical comedy.

Afterwards the dresser's daughter came backstage to see the popular star.

"Now!" said the child's mother, "tell Miss Lawrence how you liked her."

Sullen-faced the child stared at Gertrude Lawrence and said: "Yer can't dance and yer can't sing. I think you're rotten!'"

Frankness of that sort is shattering, even from a child. When the pill is sugar-coated, the sting is of course lessened. At seventy years old the French actress Mistinguette was remarkably beautiful and still had the figure of a Venus, plus the shapely gams. But at eighty she began to show her age a little.

At a dinner party in Paris she was talking to a priest, who was one of the guests. (Such social functions in France usually aim at having representatives of the Church, Law, Medicine, Politics, etc.)

The celebrated French actress said to him: "Father, I must tell you. Every morning after my bath I stand naked in front of the mirror for about ten minutes—admiring my body. Is that a sin?"

"No, Madame," the Padre replied. "It is an error."

A planned comedy of errors which turned out otherwise occurred when David Warfield and his director had some spare time on their hands in Denver where the famous actor was to appear in a play. They thought they would try to prove Shakespeare's dictum that "the play's the thing" and thus refute the theory that the star is more important than the play.

So Warfield disguised himself as an indigent vaudeville comedian, and applied for a job at one of the theaters. He did a "run-through" of a skit which he had learned in his music hall days, a thoroughly mediocre performance altogether. The ruse went over perfectly and the theater manager did not recognize him as David Warfield. But afterwards he said: "I'll engage you for a week's run, but what I want you to do is to think up an act in which you will satirize David Warfield. You have all his hammy style."

There was rivalry between David Belasco and David Warfield, both competing for the fickle mistress of Broadway. A certain talented actress remained faithful to Belasco, continually playing in his productions, and was always deaf to Warfield, who wanted her to be his leading lady. He met her one day and asked her point-blank why she circumscribed herself in this way.

"Mr. Belasco pays me well and promises me immortality," she said.

"All right," said Warfield, "I'll offer you fifty dollars a week more than Belasco pays you, and charge you nothing for immortality!"

Oscar Hammerstein once had an amazing experience with someone who wished to enter eternity in a hurry. A dishevelled and unmannerly man entered his office.

"I've got an act to offer you which you will never have the chance on again. It will take Broadway by storm, and the audience will never recover from it."

Evincing interest, Hammerstein encouraged the man with a nodding head.

"All you have to do," the man continued, "is to put twenty-five thousand dollars into escrow for my wife—and then I'll commit suicide on the stage of your theater!"

Hammerstein was by now jumpy enough, but outwardly he kept calm and collected.

"But what would we do for an encore?" he asked, as he telephoned to Bellevue Hospital.

To conclude: An English journalist was interviewing John Barrymore.

"Is it true, Mr. Barrymore, that you see pink elephants?"

"No," said Barrymore. "Pink elephants see me!"

Musical Merriment

Almost every musical artist has encountered the hostess who expects him to sing for his supper. Paderewski, the Polish master of the piano, got tired early in his career of being exploited in this way. "Why," he once asked, "does a woman think you should perform just because she gives you a dinner worth two dollars?"

In New York he was being entertained by this type of hostess. After dinner the guests assembled in the drawing room, and she asked Paderewski to play a few pieces on the piano which had been set up for the purpose.

"Oh, Madame," said the great pianist, "I haven't eaten that much of your food have I?"

On the other hand, there are those artists who have never quite arrived and who are willing to perform at a moment's notice—sometimes to the agony of those present. Music lovers will recall with mixed feelings the name of Florence Foster Jenkins, who was the proud possessor of what critics unanimously called "the worst voice in the world."

Yet she filled Carnegie Hall whenever she chose. She successfully put on concerts all over the United States, made phonograph records which sold in the thousands and made a small fortune out of it all. No one has yet decided for certain if this amazing woman was playing a joke on the public or actually took herself seriously.

In her concerts there would be offerings from classic songs of great composers to which Madame Jenkins would do violence in her inimitable manner. But before she began concertizing, her singing was largely in the parlor category. And finding that she could hold an audience (which doubtless held back its laughter), she gradually made incursions into the professional field.

Soon her fame spread far and wide, and music-lovers bought tickets so that they could go and laugh at the ridiculous antics of Madame Foster Jenkins. How she could have failed to realize the fiasco of her concertizing is hard to understand, but apparently she went to her reward (she died in 1945) believing that she was one of the "greats" of all time.

Virgil Thomson the music critic, wrote: "If I were to say what I think of this lady's voice it would be libelous. So I shall just say that I went to hear her."

At the height of her "career" Madame Jenkins was involved in a taxi accident. She was slightly injured, and to her delight she found that she could sing a truer high "C" than heretofore. So instead of suing the taxi company, she sent the driver a box of cigars.

By a natural transfer of thought, while on the subject of poor singers, Giuseppe Verdi was once scheduled to audition two singers for a forthcoming production of one of his operas. The two men appeared at his home unexpectedly and disturbed his rest. Somehow he had forgotten the appointment and, slightly disinclined to hear the men, he felt obligated to go ahead with the audition.

To add to his annoyance at having been disturbed, the singers were not of the best. To one he said: "You are the worst singer in the world!"

The other man beamed. "Then I get the role, Master?"

"No you do not," said Verdi angrily. "You can't sing at all."

It is sad but true that people of meager talent are often just as conceited as if they excelled. Mayor LaGuardia was very proud of his "musicianship." Next to his love of riding the city fire engines, he enjoyed conducting the various city department orchestras of New York.

Once he was due to conduct the New York City Sanitation Orchestra at Madison Square Garden. The officials were making a great fuss over his presence and a special room had been improvised for him to rest in beforehand.

"Please don't bother over me too much," he ordered. "Treat me as if I were Bruno Walter."

All the same LaGuardia was one of the rare personalities among public officials to know anything about music at all. Few American presidents have been musical. Of course, former President Truman can pick out a tune on the piano. When Mr. James Byrnes was Secretary of State, there was the famous gag, "Truman plays the piano while Byrnes roams."

President Ulysses S. Grant, on the other hand, had no musical pretensions whatsoever. He freely admitted that it was impossible for him to distinguish between one tune and another. Nevertheless he attended concerts and seemingly enjoyed them. At one of these, a distinguished visitor to Washington, sitting next to him, said: "I know that tune so well, Mr. President. Can you tell me its name?"

To which Grant replied: "I am sorry, but I only know two tunes. One of them is 'Yankee Doodle'—and the other isn't."

Music and men of state do not seem to mingle. President Coolidge was averse to going to concerts and attended them only when his presence was required. Whether he could carry a tune in his introspective head is not on record.

However, during a concert at the White House a soprano was doing her best with a rendition of "The Last Rose of Summer." This had been chosen so that the President's taste would not be taxed; also because it was an appropriate time of year.

"What do you think of the singer's execution?" someone asked the President.

In the agony of his frustration, the President said: "I'm all for it."

In the days of Coolidge at least music was melodious, which denotes a succession of single notes making musical sense. In so-called modern music, the accent is on the abstract. An American business man (who composed for an avocation) named Charles Ives was "discovered" as a major composer when he was nearly eighty. The music of Ives is a cacophony of dissonance, and he admitted that it was greatly influenced by his listening as a child to his father's brass band tune up. He insisted that he did not wish to please the public ear.

Anyway, Ives was a modest and retiring man, and if modern music continues to emphasize discord, he might one day be acclaimed a master of melody. As it is, he is a Pulitzer Prize winner whether he liked it or not. As a matter of fact, when told that he had been awarded the prize, Ives replied haughtily: "Give it to a waiter. It is a tip. I don't accept tips."

How fortunate he was, for most musicians are trying to think of ways to augment their incomes. Arnold Schönberg, the inventor of the twelve-tone technique of composition, was living in Hollywood during the war, a refugee from Europe. He extended a feeler to the film studios, hinting that he would like to try his hand at film music.

Finally he was offered the job of writing music for a scene in *The Good Earth*. "We want you to write some very special music," said the director of the film in the preliminary discussion. "The first few scenes will, we feel, give you a wonderful outlet for your talents."

"How so?" asked Schönberg.

"Well, you see," continued the director, chewing on his cigar. "We start with an earthquake. Think of it! The bowels of the earth open up with terrifying thunder. A hurricane is shrieking and the wind is about 90. Everyone in the scene is screaming their heads off . . ."

"But," asked Schönberg, interrupting, "why do you need my music at all?"

It is significant that some of the most successful composers cannot write a bar of music and do not even understand the thirty-two bar pattern. Irving Berlin achieved his first success in Tin Pan Alley with the aid of a musical secretary to whom he sang his songs as they came into his head.

One day, the story goes, he was in Paris and thought it was time he had some piano lessons, and the name of Stravinsky, the composer who brought about so many alterations in musical taste, was recommended. An interview was arranged, and Berlin inquired what the price of the lessons would be.

"I base my fees on what you make out of your music," said Stravinsky. "How much do you earn?"

"Oh, about one hundred thousand a year," said Berlin.

"Away with you," cried Stravinsky, "I ought to take lessons from you!"

Certainly all composers are influenced by a master of some kind or other. Brahms was affected deeply by Beethoven and he considered himself second only to that great genius. One of his friends was a leading vintner in Berlin. One day they were both celebrating a great success which a new symphony by Brahms had achieved. The vintner had taken a lot of trouble to find a very rare wine in his cellar. "It is fit for the Emperor himself," he said. "Try it, Maestro."

Brahms sampled it, smacked his lips and said: "I would like it better if it were a bottle of Beethoven!"

Tragedy has stalked the lives of some of the great composers. Hugo Wolf, the composer of some of the loveliest *lieder,* went insane at the height of his creative genius. So alienated in mind did he become that he was unable to recognize his own beautiful music. But he was still sane enough to know that he was mad!

In the asylum where he was incarcerated, he pointed to a large clock in the dining room. "Is that clock right?" he asked an attendant.

"As far as I know," answered the man.

"Then what's it doing here?" he inquired.

A similar fate was in store for Edward MacDowell, the American "poet of the piano." He lost his mind in 1906, never to regain it. But prior to that time he had a keen sense of humor.

A friend once told him that he had recently heard the composer's delicate piece, "To a Wild Rose," played by a high-school girl at an amateur concert.

"I expect she tore it up by the roots," laughed MacDowell.

All of his life MacDowell was slightly eccentric, in the tradition of great artists. An aspiring composer brought him a piece of music with the request that MacDowell comment upon it.

Not hearing further, the young man called on the composer, who was then considered America's greatest. They talked of everything except the piece of music which had been given to MacDowell to criticize. Finally, driven beyond politeness, the young man asked MacDowell outright what he thought of it.

Not answering immediately, MacDowell crossed the room to the window, put his hand outside, and brought indoors a piece of weather-beaten manuscript. Handing it to its owner, he said: "I thought it needed a little air, so I hung it outside."

In his day, MacDowell lacerated many an ego. He had a lengthy feud with Professor Nicholas Murray Butler, the President of Columbia University, which rose to the heights of vituperation. MacDowell was fighting for the proper place of music on the curriculum and the victory actually cost him his life as a composer. (Some people think that this row, which was made public, precipitated the nervous breakdown from which he never recovered.)

In one of their clashes, the famous pedagogue said: "I never pronounce on anything unless I pronounce on the facts."

In measured, majestic delivery, MacDowell replied: "That must limit your conversation a great deal."

Happily, today the Chair of Music at Columbia University is called the MacDowell Chair, a Pyrrhic victory for the composer perhaps, but mute testimony that he was in the right.

No one would ever have expected Albert Einstein to hold a Chair of Music, and yet he was a good amateur violinist. Although he undoubtedly proved that his knowledge of the instrument would never supersede his mastery of relativity, he got such friends as Hubermann to give him lessons.

One day the great master-virtuoso was working with him. "One, two, three, four. One, two, three, four," he kept repeating. But the famous mathematician was not only off key, but also off beat! They were going through a difficult piece by Mozart and Hubermann's sensitive ears were strained to the utmost. Finally, in desperation, he expostulated: "No! No! No! Albert! It's one, two, three, four! Can't you count?"

In the case of Fritz Kreisler, practicing on his precious violin is not always essential—if one can believe a story told by one of his friends.

They were travelling together by car to Paris from Berlin and Kreisler was temporarily without his violin. So he took up his friend's umbrella, and using an ash stick as a bow, he went through the entire program of his forthcoming concert. Tuning his voice like the violin itself, he sang all the pieces planned for the concert, correcting himself until he was tone-perfect in his head.

But on another occasion in London, he was spending many hours in his hotel room practicing the necessary modulations, this time on the instrument itself. And a lady occupying the adjoining suite complained to the management that she was being considerably disturbed by what she called "an abominable row" next door.

When she was politely informed by the manager that she was

actually listening to the one and only Kreisler rehearsing his concert and that she could legitimately be charged a special fee, she was full of apologies.

One of Fritz Kreisler's early concerts was given before the Sultan of Turkey at the Royal Palace in Constantinople, the same potentate with whom Augustus John had the horrifying encounter recounted in the chapter on artists.

The great violinist was doing his best to please Abdul the Second, who was surrounded with all his veiled women. But the deadpan expression of the ruler made it impossible for him to know how he was succeeding.

Kreisler was in the middle of one of Paganini's *Twenty-Four Caprices,* and was about to modulate into the most impassioned part, when the Sultan began clapping loudly. Flattered, Kreisler put all the effort for perfection which his genius alone could confer on the great music, and to his amazement the Sultan continued clapping.

After a few minutes the Grand Vizier stepped up to him. Angrily he asked: "Do you wish to lose your head? His Majesty has been trying to signal to you that he has heard enough!"

Kreisler let his bow fall to the ground and stammered as the Sultan and his ladies looked on. He tried to explain that in his experience clapping was a sign of pleasure. But all to no avail.

The Grand Vizier continued: "The last musician who continued after His Majesty gave the signal to cease was severely punished. Leave the Palace at once. You have incurred the Royal displeasure."

Later Fritz Kreisler discovered that the music of Paganini was associated with some sort of unpleasant experience in the Sultan's life and always affected him adversely.

Kreisler has described fine music as "an outburst of the soul" and when we appreciate a piece of melody we can perhaps believe that it was addressed to our soul by the composer. Unfortunately modern composers do not belong to the cult of melody—

or very few of them seem to be members. Time was when composers would raid each other's material. Rossini was asked by a composer of this type to listen to a score of music which the man had written. After the first few bars, Rossini reached for his hat and put it on his head. During the playing he raised his hat several times as if in genuflection.

"What did you keep doffing your hat for?" asked the composer afterwards.

"Well," said Rossini, "you see, I always take off my hat when I meet an old acquaintance. And every few bars in your music I recognized I had met here and there before."

A similar thing happened to Eric Coates, the English semi-classical composer. He was standing in the back of a theater with a young composer listening to a rehearsal of the young man's symphony. Suddenly he noted that several parts had been lifted from one of his famous *London Suites*.

"I must say," he smiled, "this music is *very* familiar to me!"

"Yes," said the composer, embarrassed. "All us young fellows come to you sooner or later."

As we have observed, unhappy fates sometimes await the great people associated with music. Lena Gilbert Ford, who wrote the words for "Keep the Home Fires Burning" (that stirring song which kept the flame of hope alive in England during World War I), was actually burned to death in her own home. And John Howard Payne, author of the classic song "Home Sweet Home", spent most of his life wandering abroad and finally died in a faraway land, lonely and homeless. But on one of his trips back to the U.S.A., he went to a concert where his famous song was being sung by a soprano who did violence to it.

The poet-musician wore his hair very long in consonance with his vagabond nature. After hearing his song tortured, he left the concert hall and got into a hansom cab.

"Where to?" asked the driver.

"Anywhere, anywhere!" said the distracted Payne.

"All right, we'll go to the nearest barber," said the cabbie as he hurried the horses.

Strange forms of stimuli have been needed in certain instances to put the composer in the mood for work. Borodin was unable to write a line of music unless he was feeling ill. Actually a doctor by profession and a composer by avocation, it became a habit of his admirers to greet him with: "I hope you are feeling ill today, Maestro!"

In the same vein, great music has been evolved while experimenting medically. The *Goldberg Variations* were written from a few bars by J. S. Bach under exceedingly strange circumstances. Dr. Goldberg was the personal physician for Count Keyserling (an ancestor of the man of that name referred to in the chapter on lecturing). The Count had difficulty in getting to sleep and Goldberg composed some music of a very somnolent kind for his patient, working out the sublime variations which today have the opposite effect. When played at concerts they now keep everyone wide awake with their beauty!

To be kept awake with toothache when one is a composer in the middle of a major work is unpleasant enough, but to have the wrong tooth pulled is adding insult to injury. Yet this happened to Gustav Mahler, the great Austrian composer.

Madame Alma Mahler-Werfel, his widow, recalls it all vividly. Mahler was working hard on his *Sixth Symphony* when he came down with a raging toothache. He was up all night with the nagging pain, and the next day he could do no work at all. After deciding which tooth was to be pulled, they went together to a dentist. Mahler settled himself nervously in the chair, and then an argument ensued with the dentist as to which tooth was offending. Finally Madame Mahler was called.

"Which tooth is it, Alma?" Mahler asked, nearly biting the dentist's probing finger as he did so. Madame Mahler pointed to a large molar which she and her husband had decided was the cause of all the pain. Since this was at a time before X Ray, dentists were inclined to pull teeth at random, and out came Mahler's second molar.

But the pain persisted, and Mahler was still unable to work for several days. Back at the dentist, Madame Mahler accused the man of pulling the wrong tooth. He made an examination.

"Ah," he said, "I now see which tooth must come out. We were a little hasty."

"Why can't you be more accurate?" growled the composer.

"Don't worry," said the dentist, "maybe I can make up for it by saving one of your other teeth." One way of mollifying him for the loss of his molar.

Which is a little like the story told in an Irish hospital about the gangrene patient whose wrong leg was amputated. This error was not discovered until several days after the surgery and when the doctor was informed, he replied: "Oh, yes. I have already become aware of the mistake and have just examined the patient's diseased leg. I have very good news for him. I believe it will get better."

There is always something mildly amusing about the conductor of an orchestra, and he ought to be the joy of every caricaturist. But for some reason there are few stories worth telling about conductors. Of course, there was the time Sir Thomas Beecham's gymnastics at Carnegie Hall resulted in his breaking his suspenders. After the applause had died down, he was seen to leave the podium clutching his trousers to avoid more serious embarrassment.

The brilliant British conductor aroused the ire of Melba when he was conducting her in the role of Desdemona.

"You make me die too soon," she protested.

Sir Thomas had the last word. "No opera singer dies too soon for me," was his acid rejoinder.

On one of his many trips to America, Sir Thomas was approached by the secretary of the English Speaking Union with a view to asking if he would make an appearance at one of their gatherings. "Sir Thomas," said the Secretary, in a broad American accent, "this is the English Speaking Union."

"I don't believe it," said Sir Thomas. "You must be the American Speaking Union!" And he hung up the telephone.

Speaking of Desdemona, when the Czech tenor Leo Slezak sang in *Otello* at the Metropolitan on a certain occasion with Toscanini conducting, he became ill at a critical moment. It was just at the moment when Otello has to grab Desdemona around the waist, pick her up in his arms and carry her up some steps where he must lay her down for the death scene.

In this performance Desdemona was being sung by Madame Alda who tipped the scales at well over two hundred pounds. Slezak felt that he could just manage to go on with his part and finish it if only he did not have to carry the weighty soprano. So he whispered in her ear: "I am ill tonight. Please go and die by yourself!" And Madame Alda obliged.

Another time, Leo Slezak was singing the lead in *Lohengrin*, also at the Metropolitan. In the scene where he had to make his entrance on one of the swans which is mechanically drawn across the stage, Slezak missed several which were moving too fast for him to mount.

Turning to the stagehand, he asked in the calmest manner: "Can you tell me what time the next swan leaves?"

Madame Alda was perhaps the last of those prima donnas to wear the tinsel crown which permitted temperamental outbursts. With rising costs of production, these artistic luxuries are no longer countenanced in the realm of opera.

She was once rehearsing an important operatic role under the direction of Toscanini. In a sharp exchange of words with the maestro about a matter of musical propriety, she said: "Please remember that I have plenty of musical sense."

Toscanini bowed politely. "If you had as much here," he said, touching his forehead, "as you have there"—and he placed his hand on his breast, "you'd be fortunate!"

Another great songstress who could be amusingly temperamental was Adelina Patti, whose voice thrilled music-lovers of many lands. In an argument on one occasion between her and her manager about the matter of a fee, the exasperated man interjected: "Madame Patti, you are already making more money than the President of the United States . . ."

"So get the President to sing for you!" bawled the great soprano.

The hankering for the "fast dollar" shared by many prima donnas perhaps results from their realization that what they have to sell is a perishable commodity. Madame Melba always inserted in her contracts that she must be paid more than the tenor with whom she sang. Thus on several occasions at Covent Garden she was paid five hundred pounds, while Caruso got four hundred and ninety-nine!

Backbiting and jealousy has always existed among composers. Musical history teems with feuds which have even come to the point of fisticuffs. Maeterlinck challenged Debussy to a boxing match over the question of who should sing Mélisande in the first production of *Pelléas and Mélisande*. Saint-Saëns insulted César Franck on every occasion they met. He used to tell his friends that his little pet dog would come to the piano pedals and annoy his feet whenever he played any of Franck's music, and in one of his articles he wrote:

"The word *progress* denotes something moving forward, and in moving forward you must leave something behind. Music is going forward and César Franck is being left behind. . . ."

All the same Saint-Saëns never wrote such impassioned music as Franck and posterity may veer heavily towards the latter if it should come to a choice between the two composers.

When the music of Richard Wagner began to eclipse that of Rossini, the older musician said: "Wagner's music has wonderful moments, but ghastly quarter hours."

And the German genius replied: "After Rossini dies, who will there be to promote his music?"

Critics have often been inhospitable to first performances of music which have later graduated into the masterpiece category. It took a good many years for Mascagni's opera *Cavalleria Rusticana* to win its place among the classic operas. Mascagni was wearied with waiting for his fame to come and was resolved to live in respected anonymity when it did arrive. One of his other operas called *Iris*, which did not achieve such favor, he dedicated thus: "To myself, with unalterable satisfaction!"

The revolutionary Russian composer Prokofieff, who wrote music in an idiom which he made his very own, spent the greater part of his life in exile from Russia. He returned there a few years before his death and was forced to write his music along the line of Party propaganda.

One day a Commissar said to him, trying to cheer him out of a black mood: "Think of it! One day your house will have a plaque on its front saying: 'Prokofieff lived here.'"

"Yes," said the composer sourly, "there will be a plaque—but it will read 'This house for sale.'" He was right!

... 5

Artistic Antics

More than a few good stories attest to the fact that the life of the artist "ain't all paint." Picasso has said that in order to draw well, one must learn technique and then forget it. And there are some critics who think that Picasso should learn it all over again and then remember it!

His friend Matisse, whom I met some years ago on the Côte d'Azur, was also his competitor at confounding the critics. Matisse told me the story of Picasso's divorce from his wife, who was the daughter of a Spanish general (and who felt that she had married beneath herself, even though her husband had been awarded world-wide renown).

Madame Picasso, it seems, obtained a court order which enjoined her husband from touching any of his half-finished paintings which, even in that state, were worth a fortune to his collectors. She made this move, if you please, for fear he might intentionally spoil them before the court ruling on her alimony was made.

Matisse, who himself took up painting by accident (when he was a child his mother bought him a box of paints to keep him happy during an illness), smiled shrewdly when he told me all this: "Who would have known the difference had he spoiled them or not?" he asked.

This reminded me of a story told about John Singer Sargent,

the famed portraitist, who was once asked by a friend what he thought of Cézanne.

After some consideration, Sargent replied: "I like the work of the old masters, because I can see how they've done it—and I can also see what they've done. But with Cézanne, I can see how he's done it, but I can't make out for the life of me just what he's done."

An artist who carries on in the tradition of Sargent is Augustus John, R.A., considered one of the finest living artists in England today. He is also one of the finest living storytellers, and among his own circle he is known as a purveyor of tall tales. Here is one from his repertoire.

When he was a young man, already famous, he received a commission from Abdul Hamid II, Sultan of Turkey. Rumors of an unpleasant kind had circulated throughout the world about this ruler who was deposed in 1909 for acts of cruelty and ineptness in governing his country. Significantly, after his abdication a number of human skulls were discovered weighted down at the bottom of the river outside his palace. These were believed to have belonged to some of his wives!

Upon his arrival at the Sultan's Palace, Mr. John was a little surprised to find that the Sultan wanted him to execute an anecdotal painting of the beheading of John the Baptist. Naturally he would have preferred to have done a portrait of the Sultan, whose face was an intriguing study in wickedness, but he proceeded with his orders.

During the work, the Sultan paid several visits to the studio where John was working, and on one occasion a slight argument ensued between the two men as to the appearance of the neck of Saint John after decapitation. Neither could agree, and suddenly, to the horror of Augustus John, the evil old Sultan called for one of his wives, whom he ordered to be executed on the spot.

"See how right I was?" asked the Sultan, as if nothing had happened.

"Indeed I do, Majesty," said John, as he hurried on with the painting so that he could return to London as soon as possible—and comparative safety again.

Augustus John is now a very old man and his memories stretch as far back as the times of James McNeill Whistler, whom he knew when he was a young man. And what times they were! In *The Gentle Art of Making Enemies* Whistler chronicled his many quarrels with such men as Ruskin, Swinburne and Oscar Wilde. Whistler sued Ruskin for saying that in one of his paintings he had flung a pot of paint into the public's face. He brought a libel action and was awarded one farthing damages.

This unhappy knack of turning friends into foes made his old age rather pathetic.

"I'm lonely," he sulked one day to a friend. "They are all dying. I have hardly one personal enemy left."

He once made a pencil sketch of Oscar Wilde—a hurried affair with no pretensions to being up to Whistler's usual standard.

"It's a pretty poor work of art," Wilde remarked.

"Yes. And you're a pretty poor work of nature," commented Whistler grimly.

It was a memorable event when Whistler and Mark Twain met. Both men were known to be savagely misanthropic and they stared at each other like skilled fencers. Immediately Mark went to the easel in Whistler's studio upon which stood a canvas Whistler had been painting.

"Upon my word, Whistler," said Mark Twain, "I think you and Velázquez are the two greatest painters that ever lived!"

"Why drag in Velázquez?" asked Whistler arrogantly.

Then Mark began pointing out things in the painting which struck him as interesting, bringing his gloved hand dangerously near to the wet canvas.

"For the love of God, be careful, Clemens," cried Whistler. "You don't seem to realize that the paint is fresh!"

"That's all right," said Mark, with a pleasant shake of the head. "I have my gloves on."

Whistler's studio was filled with half-finished paintings which he kept hanging on the walls. Once Sir Edwin Landseer paid him a call, and noticing the array of half-done paintings, he said: "How is it you never finish your work? I never can understand artists who leave their paintings unfinished."

"And I can never understand why you ever begin yours," said Whistler, frowning.

Of course Whistler was sometimes at the receiving end of sarcasm. One of his friendly enemies was a celebrated throat specialist who lived in Harley Street, the fashionable district for London doctors.

One day Whistler took his dog to see the specialist and asked him to examine the animal because he thought his bark was hoarse. The doctor obliged, but the next day sent Whistler a note asking him to come and paint his front door.

In Whistler we have the artist-storyteller, and those who know his work will recognize that many of his paintings are subtle stories of the emotions. On one of his commissions he was engaged to do a life-size portrait of Cléo de Mérode, a beautiful and famed French actress of her day. According to Whistler, she had elected to be painted in the nude and brought her mother with her as chaperone at each sitting.

As the work proceeded and the actress lay like a Venus upon a couch, wearing nothing but a bandeau around her lovely head, the mother was on sentry duty nearby. At one of the sittings, Whistler wanted to move the bandeau slightly higher in order to reveal the woman's ears.

Taking a few steps towards the recumbent figure, he asked if he might adjust the bandeau to the position he wished. The old harridan of a mother stopped him short: "Oh, no, no, no, Monsieur!" she cried. "My daughter's ears are for her husband."

When critics attacked Whistler, he slew them. And if foolish friends made fatuous remarks he spared them not! Such a friend came to the studio one day and told Whistler he had been spending the day on the banks of the River Thames. "I must say the scenery reminded me of some of your lovely paintings," the lady said.

"Yes," said Whistler, dryly, "Nature is improving."

The conceit of a man like Whistler calls to mind a story told about Michelangelo. At the time he was working on his great statue of Lorenzo de' Medici, a critic said: "Master, your statue is not very like him."

To which the Titan replied: "A thousand years hence, who will care whether it is like him or not?"

Rodin, the sculptor genius, had no time for small talk. A lady admirer once said to him: "Master, you make it all look so easy. Just how do you begin?"

"Yes, it is easy," said Rodin, "all you have to do is to take a large piece of marble, and with your chisel you knock away all that you don't need."

Abraham Lincoln was an intelligent judge of art. At a friend's house he was once shown a picture done by an amateur and was asked his opinion of it. "I can truthfully say," said Abe, "that the painter has observed the Commandments."

"How so?" asked the owner of the painting.

"Because," said Lincoln, "he hath not made to himself the likeness of anything in heaven above, or that which is on earth beneath, or that which is in the water under the earth."

Samuel Morse, the American inventor, was a painter of no mean order, but Lincoln didn't think so. Morse was very proud of his large canvas depicting Christ riding an ass into Jerusalem. When showing it to Lincoln, he said: "Tell me candidly, what do you think?"

Lincoln examined carefully the draughtmanship of the painting and stood back, observing, "Morse, your donkey is the savior of your picture."

However, Lincoln is on record as being an admirer of Hogarth, an artist who had a cruel wit and made enemies by the dozen with it. Once he painted a very ugly, aged peer, who was as noted for his wealth as for his parsimony. If the tiresome old man had ever taken the trouble to look in the mirror he would have seen that he resembled a monkey! But this he never did because each day he was dressed by his servants.

With the precision which was the gift of Hogarth, he portrayed an excellent likeness of the peer which was so unflattering that the old codger refused to pay for it. Hogarth felt constrained to send a note asking for payment. He wrote: "If you do not call and pay for the portrait I have made of you forthwith, I shall add a tail to it, along with other simian appendages, and will have the portrait exhibited at your club." Needless to say the matter was settled immediately.

Hogarth did not enjoy the success in his day which came later to Sir Joshua Reynolds who used to paint over two hundred portraits per year. This he achieved with the help of assistants who would wash in the backgrounds and paint the clothes and accessories of the sitters.

In his old age, Sir Joshua painted the portrait of Dr. Samuel Johnson, who was not at all pleased with the result. Johnson suffered from a weakness of the eyes, which gave him a decided squint. And Reynolds expressed this defect in the portrait more noticeably perhaps than necessary.

After seeing the portrait, Johnson complained to Mrs. Thrale, his boon companion. "It's not very friendly of Reynolds to hand down my imperfections to posterity," he growled.

Mrs. Thrale tried to mollify him. "Witness how Sir Joshua has executed his own self-portrait holding his ear trumpet," she said.

"Let him paint himself to look as deaf as he likes," he roared, "but I'm damned if I'm going to let him make me into 'Squinting Sam'!"

All chroniclers of Reynolds' life have spoken of the great artist's addiction to snuff. While painting a portrait, he would take pinch after pinch of it, inhaling it vigorously. At work on a portrait of one of the Duchesses of Marlborough, he was spilling his snuff over a fine Oriental carpet in the drawing room of Blenheim Palace. The Duchess ordered a flunkey to clean up the mess he had made, but Sir Joshua halted her. "I pray you leave the snuff alone, for the damage to your carpet will be slight compared to the dust which will settle on my canvas if it is swept up."

Thus squelched, the Duchess said nothing to Sir Joshua's face. But in her diary she recorded: "Sir Joshua is a man to be reckoned with. And he has a poor sense of personal hygiene."

Throughout the ages artists have been handicapped by the lack of time great sitters could give them. When Napoleon posed for Jacques Louis David the first time, the ruler said: "I shall give you only one sitting. After that you must rely on glimpses of me."

David was distraught. "One sitting?" he questioned. "I must have at least three, Sire."

"Nonsense," boomed Napoleon. "Do you think that Alexander bothered to pose more than once for Appelles? You should only need to look once into a face like mine to get the inspiration needed."

Which goes to prove that Napoleon had never tried his hand at portraiture and explains a cryptic statement by one of his secretaries. "The Emperor loves art," wrote Bourienne, "in the same way a butcher loves a fat ox."

David had his troubles with the Great Man in the posing of the portrait, too. "How would you like me to paint you, Sire? With sword in hand?" he asked.

"Idiot," replied the Emperor. "Victories are not won by swords. Paint me with my maps near me, like this!" And forthwith he fell into his favorite stance, with legs astride and right hand tucked in his great coat, his mind seemingly wrapped in thought.

Was he satisfied with the result? Few great men have been pleased with their likenesses. Once a friend congratulated Rodin on his life-like sculptural executions of Mercié, Falguière, and Puvis de Chavannes,—all men still living at the time. "You have made speaking-likenesses of them," the friend said.

"And would you believe it?" sighed Rodin. "Not one of those men is *speaking* to *me* any more. Each says he has been libelled!"

As he spoke, Rodin was putting the finishing touches on the bust of Geoffrey Dubois, which was being sent to the famous French writer. "Another enemy," he said as he polished a part of the marble.

Art collectors today are very friendly to the work of Rodin. One of his earliest admirers and collectors was the great J. P. Morgan, the darling of the auction galleries. Auctioneers secretly watched his markings in their catalogs as he sat in the showrooms so that they would know what his intended purchases were. Thus what he marked would mysteriously go up in price.

Soon the famous financier noticed this and took steps to fool the auctioneers. At one particular sale, the auctioneer expressed surprise that Mr. Morgan had not placed bids on certain items which he had suggested would be to his taste—but in reality his curiosity was piqued because the purchases did not tally with the markings Morgan had made in the catalog.

"You see," said Morgan casually, "today I am bidding on all the things I didn't mark."

Writing and painting are said to be the two most difficult arts if done well. The brother of William Butler Yeats, the Irish poet, is Jack Yeats, an artist who is as good with his brush and palette as the poet was with his pen and paper. But the last time they met, the poet was feeling very ill. "How I envy you your healthy body, Jack!" he said sadly.

And Jack, recalling the incident, adds: "He never said anything about me mind."

In his student days Jack Yeats lived in London where he studied at the Slade School of Art. He resided in a boarding house which was run by a very prudish woman, who objected to some nude studies which the artist was working on. So Jack was forced to pin paper drawers on the nudes in order to keep the good lady happy.

The Slade School of Art was at that time headed by Alphonse Legros, a French artist of considerable renown. Upon his appointment to the school, he took out British citizenship as an act of courtesy. Naturally other French artists made gibes at his defection and one of them asked him forthrightly what he expected to gain by his change in nationality. Legros smiled wryly: "To begin with, I win the battle of Waterloo!"

Waterloo was Napoleon's sunset and who could paint sunsets better than Joseph Mallord Turner? He never missed the chance of watching a sunset; thus he knew more about them than most artists. One day at his studio an art critic was pausing at the sight of one of these exquisite paintings.

"It's very fine, Mr. Turner," he said, "but I must confess that I have never seen a sunset as beautiful as that one."

"Perhaps not," replied Turner crossly, "but don't you wish you had?"

There are always people to find fault with the finest painting. A story is told about Salvador Dali, the brilliant Spanish artist, who is a great technician. Some of his paintings are indeed controversial, but no matter what the critics say, his work always has plenty of attention value.

It is said that he was standing near one of his latest paintings at a Paris exhibit and a viewer, not knowing he was Dali, said:

"What a dreadful piece of artistry!"

"I'm sorry you think that," said Dali frigidly. "It's mine."

"Do you mean to say you bought it?"

"No," replied Dali, "I painted it."

"Oh, sorry," the viewer apologized. "Please excuse me. I'm only repeating what people have said whom I have overheard talking about it."

Such highly successful artists as Salvador Dali can afford to laugh at this sort of experience. Why do not more artists reach the same dizzy heights of fame and fortune? Here are a few reasons given to me by some of the failures:

They would not lower themselves to please the public taste.

Their integrity will not allow them to give the public what it wants.

The critics are against them.

They are living in advance of their time.

(The truth: They can't paint!)

... 6

Social Satire

Juvenal's social satire changed the customs of Rome! In England
Dean Swift altered the political aspect with his scathing sarcasms
and Cervantes laid to final rest the tiresome knight-errantry of
Spain. If Bernard Shaw had been born in Germany there might
never have been an Adolf Hitler! The great Irish humorist had
that highly individualistic gift of being able to make people laugh
at themselves, and a few Shavian withering remarks might have
forced Hitler off the political scene.

In today's society people meet too often. There is never enough
time allowed so that they can accumulate value to each other. The
social whirligig of New York is a good example. It has become
like a hornet's nest with its intrigues and petty feuds, nobody
knowing who is speaking to whom. I must confess that I have had
a better time at a good Irish wake than at the average cocktail
party, with all its senseless, strident conversation.

There was a time when society was more exclusive than it is
today, when the social atmosphere was decorous! Victorian gentlemen kept on their white gloves while dining and the ladies would
wear more clothes when swimming in the ocean than they did at
the opera. The tallyho of the hansoms could be heard in the avenues of New York, and life flowed with persiflage and wit.

Where are the social wits today? Once, within living memory, there was Harry Lehr, known as "King" Lehr of the Four Hundred, who said of one of the Queens of American Society: "She tries so hard to be a *grande dame* and only succeeds in being damned grand."

To a tiresome and socially ambitious dowager who was noted for the sparseness of her table, he made a witty retort.

After the "dinner" the lady said: "Now that the ice is broken between us, Mr. Lehr, and you have dined with me, I hope you'll ask me to one of your dinner parties."

"Certainly, Madame," said Lehr. "How about this evening?"

Those were the days when the New York Four Hundred would repair to such resorts of impenetrable exclusiveness as Newport, Rhode Island, ruled over by Mrs. William K. Vanderbilt and her ladies-in-waiting.

Just before the start of the European war in August 1914, this good lady had invited, rather unwisely, Count Bernstorff, the German Ambassador. She had issued her invitation to him well in advance, in keeping with diplomatic custom; but when war was declared between England and Germany a few days before his visit, Mrs. Vanderbilt prayed that he would have the discretion to excuse himself.

However, Count Bernstorff had decided to brazen it out, as it were. He turned up complete with valet and private secretary! Naturally everyone was anxious to broach the subject about the world conflagration which his ruler had started, but instead His Excellency talked about the joy of being at the seaside and other banalities.

At dinner on the evening of his arrival, things were made even tenser because of a long and embarrassing delay after the soup course. As a matter of fact, the Ambassador had taken one spoonful and, after making a grimace, ate no more of it.

Mrs. Vanderbilt became visibly nervous as the delay continued, knowing that her servants were either French, Belgian, or English. In fact, word had already reached her of agitation downstairs in the servant's hall over the distinguished guest.

After further delay, the English butler appeared and, with exaggerated hauteur, handed his mistress a note. It was signed by the chef, a patriotic Frenchman, and ran as follows: "The staff and myself have decided that we cannot serve the dinner tonight. We find it impossible to wait on a man who represents the enemy of our respective countries. We are now packing our things and will be on our way by the time you read this. I trust that your German friend found the soup to his liking. I took the liberty of adding an emetic to it."

The successor as undisputed Queen of the Four Hundred was Mrs. Cornelius Vanderbilt, whose first name was Grace—hence she became nicknamed "Her Grace." She had her servant troubles, too. Once she obtained what she thought was the perfect parlor maid. Then one day the maid gave notice without warning. She had seemed to like the work and no one could understand why she had decided to leave.

When told of the young woman's decision, Mrs. Vanderbilt sent for her. "Why do you wish to leave, Florence?" she asked, with a pained expression on her face. "Is anything wrong?"

"Yes," answered Forence. "I just can't stand the suspense in this house."

"Suspense? What do you mean?"

"You see Madame," the maid continued respectfully, "over my bed is a sign which says: 'Watch ye. For ye know not when the master cometh.' "

Mention that Mrs. Vanderbilt's nickname was "Her Grace" brings to mind the story told in England about Lady Mountbatten, wife of England's First Lord of the Admiralty. She was training a new maid.

"Now, Emma," she said, "I am expecting a friend to tea, the Duchess of So-and-So. I wish you to tell her that I will be a few

minutes late. Ask her to wait for me and show her into the drawing room. And don't forget to say 'Your Grace.' "

When the Duchess arrived the maid delivered her little speech
all right. And with Lady Mountbatten's last instruction to say
"Your Grace" ringing in her ears, she made a little curtsey, saying: "And may the Lord make us truly thankful."

In these days of dereliction by servants, the story is hard to
credit, but is also too charming to omit. I have often thought that
I might write a book and call it *Servants I Have Waited On*. Even
if one is lucky enough to find a factotum, it does not mean that
much work will be done.

Take the experience of Prince Ali Kahn (once the husband
of Rita Hayworth). Some time ago the prince was in Hollywood
and was in search of a valet. He happened to inquire of the attendant in the Gentleman's Room of a fashionable Beverly Hills
hotel if he knew of one.

The attendant became thoughtful and then made a reply which
clarifies once and for all the servant situation in California. He
said: "Actually I'm looking for a valet for myself." (For those un-
aware of it, large sums are paid for the rest-room concessions in
fashionable hotels. Only someone with ample means could afford
the job!)

Fortunately for the English, the family "retainer" is still in
existence. This type of servant remains with a family throughout
the years, knowing that he or she will be taken care of until the
grave. An amusing story is told about a butler of a prominent
titled family who was awarded the D.S.O. (a decoration second
only to the Victoria Cross) for conspicuous bravery in the field
of battle.

Lady So-and-So, his employer, was so proud of him that she
asked if she might accompany him to the investiture ceremony at
Buckingham Palace, where he was to receive the medal from King
George VI himself.

Driving the lady in the family motor car to the gates of the

Palace, the policeman stopped him, demanding to see the pass. "Sorry," he said, "this pass if only for one."

The butler tried to explain: "You see this is my mistress and she wants to see me get the D.S.O."

"Your mistress?"

"Yes, I . . ."

"Haven't you got your signals crossed? This is Buckingham Palace, not a seaside hotel!" Of course, after a clarification, the lady was permitted to pass through.

Many language misunderstandings are due to differences of intonation, as Irvin S. Cobb discovered when he went to London. At a ball he was dancing with a society dowager who was a mountain of warm flesh. After a few whirls round the floor, she said: "I can't dance any more. I'm too danced out."

"Oh, no!" Cobb countered. "Just nice and plump!"

One can visualize the askant look on the face of the lady just as vividly as one can imagine the amusement of the great humorist when he was being entertained in one of the southern states by a good-hearted hostess trying to be too refined. When asked the part of the chicken he would prefer, Cobb said: "I'll take the breast."

"I beg your pardon!" said the hostess. "Bosom, you should say."

Never at a loss for a witticism, Cobb made one of his most appropriate *bon mots* at a social gathering where Mrs. Minnie Maddern Fiske, the great American actress, arrived late. The guests were all seated in the drawing room where a singer was going to perform, and there was not one chair left. Cobb himself was standing. "You see, dear lady!" he said. "Even here there is not a seat to be had when you appear."

A story he told about one of the famous Gibson girls (who were immortalized by Charles Dana Gibson in portrait form and all of whom married titled men or millionaires) is worth repeating. The lady in question had received no formal education, but always managed to impress her gentlemen friends with her erudition. The secret of it all was that she studied the *Encyclopedia Britannica* in her bath the evening of her dinner dates.

On one occasion she was dining with a purple-faced English colonel who asked her what she thought of a certain subject. Her abashing reply was: "I really can't say. I haven't come to Z yet."

I myself had a similar experience not long ago. Seated next to a dull companion at a dinner party, I asked her what she thought of euthanasia, which was then in the news since the practice of voting death for oneself in case of hopeless illness had been just legalized in Russia. My effort to raise the standard of talk met with a flabbergasting reply: "Oh, I'm interested in youth anywhere!" said my dinner companion.

Tommy Manville, the heir to asbestos millions (yet he gets burned romantically more than any man), is apt to marry the type of woman who is beautiful but dumb. He was greeted by George Jessel (who marries them beautiful but young) with: "Please ask me to your next wedding." That was at the time when their marriages were running neck to neck.

Another time Jessel said to Tommy: "I hear you are the worst lady-killer in town."

And Tommy was equal to him: "I hope you aren't going to take away my reputation, George."

One of the noted playboy's wives is supposed to have written to him just at the time when things were cooling off between them:

"I write to you, dear, because I have nothing else to do (there followed an account of her daily doings). And I end this letter because I have nothing to say."

The history of the American playboy sums itself up in the career of Tommy Manville. Lately, the young millionaires have taken to theatricals, and there is Huntington Hartford who has spent a fortune making his wife, Marjorie Steel (a former hat-check girl), into an actress.

Many pretty young women have found matrimony a passport

into what is called (and without any justification whatever) the "aristocracy." One such young woman was brought over from Europe to "try out" for the movies. During her screen-test (she didn't get the part), she had an altercation with the director. "I'll have you know, I'm a lady," she said emphatically.

"All right," said the director, "I'll keep your secret."

Nowadays one hears a great deal about Café Society (dubbed by someone "Cafeteria Society"), reigned over by that social phenomenon Elsa Maxwell, whose success will never be completely explained.

Among the several theories of how her friendship burgeoned (and later drooped) with the Duke of Windsor there is the following. Elsa was staying at Biarritz where the Duke was holidaying with his Duchess. Neither of them had met Miss Maxwell, but that was not for want of trying on her part. She was determined to meet His Royal Highness, and she hit on a plan.

One day she mooted to her friends that she had succeeded in capturing him for a dinner party. All of them wondered how this could be, since they knew Elsa did not even enjoy a speaking acquaintance with him.

As the date for the proposed party drew near, Elsa spied the Duke alone one day on the sea-front. She barged up to him: "You must know who I am!" she said coyly. "I'm Elsa Maxwell and I've made a bet with friends that I can capture you for dinner tomorrow night. The bet is rather large, and if I lose I'm ruined. Will you please, please come?"

The Duke was so amused at the brashness of it all that he accepted—although later he had a hard time persuading the Duchess to go. Thus the friendship was born, fated to end in debacle. From the start there was a personality conflict between the Duchess and Elsa. At a later party, to which she invited the Windsors, she ordered everyone to come in the guise of the person they most detested.

The Duchess didn't turn up, nor did she allow the Duke to go, although they had both accepted. Always brutally frank, Wally scored her first strike against Elsa, who asked her why she had not come to the party.

With just a hint of levity, she said: "You see, Elsa, if I had followed your instructions, I would have had to come as yourself. And I'm too slim for that!"

"That would have been all right," chirped Elsa nonchalantly. "I could have loaned you a pillow and one of my Molyneux dresses."

Which was, after all, the only answer she could make. Nothing is so disarming as humility, and Elsa Maxwell possesses this quality. Years ago there was the counterpart of this extraordinary woman, an early Elsa Maxwell, who ran the Bohemian world of Paris with an iron hand. As is true of Elsa, everyone respected her for her wit and for her organizing ability.

One day Oscar Wilde was introduced to her by Frank Harris, when the two men were strolling in the Rue de la Paix.

"Oh, Mr. Wilde," she said, "I have heard so much about you. Perhaps you have heard of me? I am the ugliest woman in Paris."

Wilde, the aesthete, took another look at her. "No, Madame!" he murmured, "you are the ugliest woman in all the world!"

As an example of Wilde's virtuosity as a society wit, Sarah Bernhardt appeared at an important London function and asked Wilde, who was also present, to get her a chair: "You are a jewel!" said the Divine One.

"No," Wilde replied, "I am a jeweller! I have set the jewel."

Many a humorous mistake is made by an unthinking journalist. In reporting the marriage of Sir Joseph Duveen, the famous art dealer, a London daily paper announced: "The marriage between Sir Joseph Duveen to Miss Elsa Salaman took place yesterday. Sir Joseph is the well-known collector of antiques."

Lord Duveen, as he later became, made a fortune out of selling *objets d'art* to millionaires, and made the bald statement that in his opinion millionaires bought at least one famous art treasure for one reason only. They were tired of being treated indifferently by their wives and children, who invariably talked back to them. The art masterpiece was something in their lives which could be admired and would not talk back! Such are the vagaries of the society millionaire!

Social letters of condolence and congratulation are always a bore to write. Talleyrand, a very busy man, worked out a solution and became known as the shortest letter-writer in France. When his niece wrote to him from Italy that she was getting married, he sent her a card saying: "Hourra! Hourra! Hourra! Votre oncle Talleyrand."

However, a short time later, the niece was bereaved of her husband and so Talleyrand then wrote: "Hélas! Hélas! Hélas! Votre oncle Talleyrand."

Not long after this, the niece wrote again, saying that she had met the man of her dreams and was getting re-married. Talleyrand dispatched a card with the words: "Ah! Ah! Ah! Votre oncle Talleyrand."

This gift for succinct communication is rare nowadays and most people deal in circumlocution. Frankness is the keynote of Winston Churchill's personality in politics and he carries it into social intercourse.

When he was forced to cancel an engagement to spend a weekend with some old friends, he wired: "Sorry. Can't come. Lying excuse follows."

Thomas Edison was very deaf in later years but revelled in thus not being forced to hold society chatter. The great inventor helped to perfect the hearing aid which is in common use today. But he would never use it himself. When asked his reason, he replied: "I'm always too busy to listen to people talking. Besides my wife would never stop asking me questions."

Deafness can lead to embarrassing situations. Once Sir John

Lavery, the Irish artist, and his wife were attending a social function in Washington and in giving her name to the butler, who was slightly deaf, Hazel Lavery said: "I am Lady Lavery."

The butler's eyes stole shyly in the direction of the powder room: "First door on the right, Madame," he said.

To be mistaken for a butler when one is American Ambassador is a galling thing, yet it happened to Joseph H. Choate, who represented the United States at the Court of St. James prior to the First World War.

It was at a Royal Levy, where almost all the Ambassadors wear very elaborate clothes, but the American tradition had been long established that ambassadors wore black evening dress. One of the departing guests mistook Mr. Choate for a flunkey. "Call me a cab, please," he ordered peremptorily.

Choate was flabbergasted, but his nimble wit, for which he was famous, did not fail him: "All right. You are a cab, Sir! How is that?"

The Englishman walked off in a huff and registered a complaint. Finally a member of the Royal Household arrived on the scene and the matter was cleared up. The Englishman offered the American Ambassador an apology. But Choate didn't let him off too easily. "You see," he said mildly, "if you were a good-looking man I would have called you a hansom cab."

By a natural transfer of thought, Choate School is one of the institutions run especially for sons of society Americans. A good many years ago, it is said, they had there at one time an Astor, a Rockefeller, and a Vanderbilt. The junior Rockefeller had been given a small boat by his father so that he could learn rudimentary navigation. Now, the Rockefellers are known for their frugality, and the boat was smaller than those of the other boys. One of the masters commented on this. "Heavens," said the young man, "do you think we're Vanderbilts?"

Among American Society millionaires the name of Charles M. Schwab is outstanding. He may not have gone to Choate School, but he had a private tutor by the name of Andrew Carnegie who taught him much that he could never learn at any school. One thing he tried continually to impress on the young Schwab was not to rest on his laurels, that success is a challenge, etc. One day Schwab sent Carnegie a telegram about some business he had been conducting abroad: "Have broken all records today." To which the Scotch money-maker wired back: "How about tomorrow?"

Upon his retirement, Schwab settled down on a luxurious plantation in the South and spent his last years there. He had a penchant for large birds which he collected, and one of these was an emu which had the run of his plantation. Once when leaving for a business conference in New York, he asked his superintendent to advise him about the bird because it seemed poorly.

Sometime later the servant sent him a telegram. "The emu has laid an egg, and in the absence of yourself I have put it under the largest goose I can find."

In passing I must make mention of a funny situation in which I became involved while visiting Field Marshal Lord Alexander and his wife at their home near London. I motored there to have luncheon with them, and as I emerged from my car, a huge dog appeared in the driveway. Dogs always made a dead set for me, and I wasn't worried when it began jumping around and wagging its tail. But I did feel some concern when it followed me to the doorway and walked in as if it owned the house.

A family pet, I felt sure, as it settled down to a corner of the living room as Lord and Lady Alexander greeted me warmly. At luncheon the dog settled down at my feet and the begging for food began. Taking a piece of meat from my plate, I threw it away from me. Lady Alexander's attention became riveted upon me:

"Mr. Mahony," she said charmingly, "I wish you would send your dog outside."

And not until then did it dawn upon me that they thought the stray dog was mine!

Mistaking the owner of a dog is not as bad as getting mixed up over the identity of a man's wife, especially if she happens to be the Duchess of Westminster.

She and the Duke moved house and baggage to Ireland after the war in order to avoid English austerity. Ireland was doubtless chosen because they could get no further abroad due to monetary restrictions. Being the richest living Englishman (he has since gone to his heavenly reward), the Duke leased an appropriate Irish castle.

The Duke and Duchess were staying one week at the leading hotel in Galway City where the horse races are an important social event in Ireland each year. Unexpectedly one day a man arrived on important business to see the Duke, and not knowing him even by sight, asked the manager to arrange for him to be escorted to the Duke at the race track.

The manager ordered the hotel porter to take him there, and without delay the porter pointed out the Duke, who was standing in an enclosure, binoculars in position for the next race. His wife, wearing a bright red hat, was by his side.

"Is that the Duchess with His Grace?" asked the business man out of curiosity.

"Ach, Sir," said the porter in his delicious brogue. "I'm not sure of that. But I do know that His Grace slept last night with the lady standing next to him wearing the red hat."

Fortunately most servants are more tactful. During the shooting season in Scotland, Sir Anthony Eden took his son to stay with some friends for the weekend.

The first day Sir Anthony was unable to accompany the boy and remained immured in his room with work. Later the butler announced that the party had returned.

"How many grouse did my son get?" he asked eagerly.

"I believe your son shot wonderfully," said the butler suavely. "But God was merciful to the birds."

Weekend guests have been known to remain longer than their

invitation, which can be a bore. Lady Mendl had a clever solution to this problem. If a guest remained over the deadline, her butler would hand the guest a railway timetable!

Lady Mendl was a society hostess who was always sure of her authority. After one of her famous parties, a certain titled lady who disliked her intensely said: "So sorry, my dear! But I completely forgot your party last week!"

"Oh!, weren't you there?" asked the witty American hostess ingenuously.

There is nothing more disenchanting than for an invitation to be tendered too near the date of a party. When a certain London hostess, who lived opposite to Sir Osbert Sitwell, asked him to a large gathering a couple of days before the event, Sir Osbert declined:

"I am sorry I cannot come to your party," he wrote. "But won't you come to tea with me the day before yesterday?"

Today of course Sir Osbert Sitwell is lionized, and he probably turns down more invitations than he accepts. The most lionized man in the world at one time was Albert Einstein, and during the early days of his fame he allowed himself to be what he called "table decoration." Fully aware that he was being used by lion-hunting hostesses, he would go to "feeding-time at the Zoo," an apt expression which he used for formal dinner parties.

On one of these occasions in Los Angeles, his hostess led him onto the balcony of her home where could be seen the stars studding the heavens of a perfect summer night.

"I can spot Venus," she said pointing towards one of the stellar bodies. "It always shines like a beautiful woman."

Einstein gazed at the brightest star. "I'm sorry to tell you that the star you mean happens to be Jupiter."

"Oh, Dr. Einstein!" the woman gushed. "No wonder they call you the world's greatest mathematician. You can calculate the sex of a star millions of miles away!"

At social functions among the film colony in Hollywood one

can sometimes almost slice the air, so thick is it with teeming jealousy. The one and only Mrs. Patrick Campbell rattled them all up nicely. Upon being presented to Mary Pickford she said: "Oh, how pretty you are! Such lovely golden hair—and from whom do you inherit those lustrous eyes?"

"Well," said Miss Pickford, flattered exceedingly, because she was well aware that Mrs. Campbell did not often make pleasant remarks to people, "I owe it all to my mother."

"Let me give you some advice," continued Mrs. Campbell in a motherly tone. "You should try to get into the movies!"

Mary Pickford reeled a little, then steadied herself:

"I am Mary Pickford!" she said with emphasis.

"Oh, well," replied Mrs. Campbell consolingly. "You could change your name."

This line of insult was followed by Stella Campbell whenever the chance presented itself, and finally a certain wit of the movies was allocated to take her down—an actress now retired from the screen.

At a party it was arranged that she should be introduced to the famous Englishwoman, and her speech was carefully rehearsed:

"Oh, Mrs. Campbell," she said, "I've been eating your soups for years, and I think they are delicious!"

Mrs. Campbell raised her eyebrows and said crushingly: "Of course—bean soups, my dear. I can tell by the sallow color of your skin!"

Which riposte was almost equalled by Israel Zangwill, the famous Jewish author and playwright. He was being entertained by some society dowagers in Chicago prior to a Zionist meeting at which he was going to speak. At luncheon he horrified his hostess by ordering roast ham.

"Mr. Zangwill," she said, "don't you see anything else on the menu which you prefer?"

"No, I want the dish I have ordered. I like roast ham."

"But," persisted the woman, "after all, we are going to a Zionist meeting, and you know the dietary laws of our religion as well as anyone."

"Madame," said Zangwill, "I have ordered ham because I like it, and, I may say, I like it a lot better than your Chicago tongue."

Zangwill possessed an incisive wit. Once after a party in Brighton, a seaside resort (where he was attending a conference), he met a fellow guest on the front. The man was a *nouveau riche* peer who did not have an "h" to his name. He was feeling the effects of the night before, sitting on a bench, his hand clapped over his forehead:

"Oh, my 'ead! My 'ead!" the man moaned.

"What you need is two aspirates," said Zangwill, consolingly.

Royal Roundup

It has been said that the war changed everything—everything, perhaps, excepting the cupidity and stupidity of man! Empires have disappeared and several thrones have been trampled in the dust! In fact today several kings are in search of other employment than kingship.

By way of commencement, to quote from the one and only Duke of Windsor: "It seems I'm becoming commoner and commoner." Doubtless he meant that he was changing with the times. But is he? To some observers he would seem to demand as much of the royal prerogatives as if he were still on the throne.

Surely his marriage to Mrs. Simpson presupposed a certain amount of adjustment? Both of them have faced all sorts of embarrassing situations, not least of which being a party given in their honor by some *nouveau riche* New Yorkers. The hostess beamed with pleasure when the Duke graced her apartment with his presence.

Taking him by the hand and leaving Wally to her own devices, she roundly addressed the assembly of guests: "Listen friends! This is the Duke of Windsor."

And with a wave of her hand towards his Duchess, she stated baldly: "*That's* Mrs. Windsor."

Most people have forgotten that there was an early Wally

Simpson in the person of Betsy Patterson of Baltimore. She married Jerome Bonaparte, brother of Napoleon I. But he abandoned her to marry a princess of Württemberg, and the persistent Betsy spent the rest of her life trying to have her child recognized as a royal son of the House of Bonaparte.

A good retort is recorded in her favor. While she was dining with the Duke of St. Albans in London, a very haughty Englishman, also a guest, said to Betsy: "I hear you are an American, Mrs. Bonaparte. I know very few of your race, but the few I have met I must say have been vulgarians."

Betsy became like a coiled snake, ready to strike, for she was very proud of being American.

"That shouldn't be surprising to you, sir! After all, we Americans are descended from your ancestors and doubtless that accounts for our vulgarity."

Returning to the House of Windsor: as the very young Prince of Wales, Edward VIII was a very bright lad. Once he was in need of money when he was at school. He knew he could always rely on sympathy from his grandmother Queen Alexandra and so he wrote to her for the loan of a pound or two. Her Majesty replied with a warning about the dangers of borrowing money and admonished the lad for not keeping his expenditures within his pocket-money allowance.

Some time later the Prince wrote back: "Dear Granny: I no longer need the loan because I sold your signature to one of my school mates for five pounds. Thanks all the same."

He developed an eye for a pretty girl very young, too. Once at a gathering where he and his brother (who later became George VI) were making a public appearance, he danced freely with the village maidens.

His brother, a stiff and shy young man of seventeen, upbraided him. "What will Grannie say?" he asked.

"Leave me alone," said Edward. "If you don't like my conduct, go over in that corner and sing *God Save my Grandmother*."

In those days he seemed to enjoy informality. On his world tour when he was in Australia, he was out cantering on horseback one day near Sydney. The groom accompanying him became alarmed at the reckless way the Prince was riding (he had so many falls that there was actually a song composed: "The British Son Never Sets on Horses"), but the good man was not sure how to address him.

"Slow down, Sir!" he yelled. "If you don't look out, you're going to break your royal neck!"

And there was the amusing encounter with the wife of a bear-trapper in Northwest Canada to whom he was introduced. She was an admirer of Queen Mary and wished to inquire about her. But she was at a loss as to the correct terminology.

"Tell me, Your Royal Highness," she asked respectfully, "how is your Ma?"

At first the Prince did not seem to follow. "Do you mean the Queen, my mother?"

"I guess she is the Queen *and* your Ma," said the woman.

"As far as I know, Madame, Her Majesty, Queen Mary, is in the best of health," answered the Prince stiffly.

At about that time the Prince purchased a ranch in Alberta province and took an interest in farming it. Once, in America, he met Henry Ford, who referred to the ranch.

"You may know, Your Highness," said Ford, "that I manufacture the best tractor in the world and I would like to make a gift to Your Highness of a couple of them."

"Indeed, I would like to try out your tractors, Mr. Ford," said the Prince, "but I would insist on paying for them."

"That would hurt my feelings, Your Highness!" exclaimed Ford.

"Not as much as it would hurt my reputation if I accepted all the things offered me for advertising purposes," smiled the heir to the British Throne.

Everyone admired the mother of the Prince of Wales for her

stateliness and personal charm. But not everyone thought so highly of Queen Mary's taste in hats. One day she was reviewing some troops at Aldershot, and the band was playing some appropriate music of the incidental type.

Her Majesty suddenly recognized, or thought that she recognized, one of the pieces. It sounded very familiar and went round and round in her head. But for the life of her she could not think of its name.

"Please make inquiries," she ordered an equerry, "for the name of that tune." And she hummed its infectious melody.

Greatly embarrassed, the equerry returned, blushing. "The name of the tune you inquired about Ma'am," he said, struggling to keep control of himself, "is *Where Did You Get That Hat?*"

It is said that Queen Mary's favorite son was Prince George, who later became the Duke of Kent and was killed flying during the war. At the time of his marriage to Princess Marina of Greece, a man named Hoare-Belisha was Minister of Transport. This shrewd man knew the value of publicity and his name was on everyone's lips. He erected a street-crossing beacon and named it the Belisha Beacon and he toiled in other ways to get himself known politically.

When Princess Marina of Greece came to England she heard a lot of references to Hoare-Belisha and was finally led to inquire: "And does my George know this whore, Belisha?"

The finest king ever to occupy the throne of any country was King George V of England. In the words of Joseph H. Choate, American wit and former Ambassador to the Court of St. James: "He did not reign, he sprinkled." With his modesty and loftiness of mind, was it any wonder that he was known as the "First Gentleman of Europe"?

His constant devotion to duty struck the imagination of the English public. One day after a shooting party in the depths of the country, he was returning on foot with his friend the Duke of Buccleuch. A farmer in his pony-cart passed by and offered the two men a lift. Being tired they accepted, and the King sat in front with the driver, the Duke of Buccleuch behind.

After a while the driver whispered to King George: "Who's your friend, Sir?"

"The Duke of Buccleuch," answered the King.

"And who may you be?" asked the curious driver, certain that he was being kidded.

"I happen to be your King," the monarch said meekly.

This made the farmer chuckle. "Then I'm the Shah of Persia," he scoffed.

It is said that the King told this story over and over to his friends. Despite his reputation for never smiling, he did have a sense of humor. This is illustrated in a story told about his one great sensibility, that of being a short man. A book of American memoirs by Colonel House was being re-published in England and, as the King was mentioned, the publisher sent him the galley-proofs for "vetting." The Colonel had referred to the King as "that bellicose little monarch," and spoke of how vehement he had been in the conduct of the war. His Majesty returned the galleys with only one deletion. He crossed out the adjective "little."

An anecdote is related about an outing he had with Andrew Mellon when he was Ambassador to Great Britain. They were driving along the banks of the River Thames and Mellon observed that it could not be compared to any of the important rivers in the United States. "Your Majesty," he said, probably trying to get a rise out of the King, "this little river of yours would be swallowed up by our Hudson."

"No doubt you are right, Mr. Mellon," said the King. "But that stretch of water you see there is more than just a river to us. We think of it as liquid history."

King George's father, King Edward VII, exercised the royal prerogative in the strictest sense, and was not one to hold back his opinion of others.

When dealing with a bumptious minister who used the royal pronoun "We" in his presence with an unroyal connotation, he said: "Only two people are permitted to refer to themselves as "We": a King, and a man with a tape-worm inside him."

The imperiousness of his grandmother Queen Victoria was well known. When one of her courtiers told her that Gladstone was saying unkind things about her, she replied: "It doesn't matter a whit what he thinks of me. It's what I think of him that is important."

How shocked the old Queen would be were she alive to have witnessed the conduct of some of her cousins. Within living memory Tsar Ferdinand of Bulgaria ruled his country by blackmail. He kept a card-index file on every member of the government so that he could refer quickly to the best way to use pressure on them.

Even Kaiser Wilhelm II, whose own record was none too good, said of him: "He's a low, cunning clown. He ought to be in jail, and if I ever catch him in Germany, I shall put him there."

Queen Victoria never took any nonsense from Wilhelm II. Once at a full-dress military review when the Kaiser was visiting England officially, he was taking the salute with the Queen nearby. He was on horseback next to the Queen's carriage and an embarrassing thing happened. One of the cavalry officers accidentally frightened the Kaiser's horse, causing it to bolt. His Majesty was badly jostled, but no visible harm was done to him.

Furious at being tossed about and exposed as a poor horseman, he said to Queen Victoria: "I demand that the careless officer be reprimanded. You should have him court-martialled."

"Don't be silly, Willie," said the Queen, chidingly. "You always were a poor seat on a horse, and you know it!"

It was Queen Victoria who did her best to make England an educative center for royalty from all over the world. In her reign, potential potentates or sons of kings were encouraged to come to the famous public schools (which are anything but public) and to the Universities of Oxford and Cambridge.

There was often a round dozen of future rulers at Eton College alone. The eldest son of the King of Siam was there in the Nineteen Twenties, a slim, shy youth who held himself aloof from the other scholars.

One day a master, trying to make friends with the lad, asked him how many brothers and sisters he had. The Prince had not been long away from his country, where it would be considered very impertinent to ask such a question (in almost every country except England and America it is bad taste to ask personal questions). He hedged and tried to avoid the answer, but when pressed again, he squelched the master with: "Who am I to know how many sons and daughters my father has sired himself."

Which makes one think of the story of the Eastern Amir who said to his daughter: "The only pleasure I have had out of you was in begetting you!"

Entertaining potentates from abroad is an everyday affair in England, where everything is done to please the royal visitor for political reasons. *Carte blanche* is given for the ruler to go to the best shops in London and charge everything to the British Exchequer.

His Majesty, the King of Afghanistan (famous for his edict removing the veils from the faces of his women subjects), came on one of these spending sprees and did himself and his Queen proudly. But the British Government got reciprocal treatment in the form of concessions and everyone was satisfied.

That is to say, everyone except the Prime Minister, Mr. Bonar Law, who had the unfortunate duty of escorting the King and Queen to certain functions. One of these was a concert in honor of the royal pair.

In the interval Mr. Bonar Law happened to ask the King which piece of music he preferred. Without taking time to consider the

matter, the King insisted that it was the first piece on the program which had pleased him most. So the Prime Minister sent
word to the conductor of the orchestra to re-play it.

This was done, but after a few bars of the music, the King of
Afghanistan shook his head negatively. No. This was not the
piece which had pleased him most. It was the very first piece
which had been played. And then comprehension dawned upon
Mr. Bonar Law that the King was referring to the orchestral tune-
up.

Quickly he sent a second message to the orchestra leader, who
scratched his head when he got it, but carried out the request.
And as notes collided and fell to the ground and half-notes
jarred in a hideous dissonance, the King's face creased into a
smile. This was indeed the music which suited his Asiatic taste.

A successor of Mr. Bonar Law got into similar difficulties when
His Royal Highness, the Paramount Chief of the Gold Coast,
came to visit England. Mr. Ramsay MacDonald, who was then
Prime Minister, was in office when this colorful visitor paid a
state call on the country. Wherever he went, this African potentate was paced by a boy slave who held over the royal head an
umbrella (the symbol of office).

An ulterior object of his visit to England was to urge the English to import more of the chief product of his country, cocoa.
Long ago the British Government had sequestered all his gold
fields and the Chief was determined to make the English take
more of his cocoa than they had in the past. So he hit on a good
publicity stunt. While in England he carried constantly a box of
chocolates made with the Gold Coast product, which he proffered
to everyone whom he met.

On the several occasions when Ramsay MacDonald had the
job of attending the Chief at certain functions in his honor, a
very embarrassing situation arose. Mr. MacDonald had an aver-
sion to sweetmeats. The Chief would offer the hated chocolates

and the Prime Minister would sneak a few of them into his pocket.

But the Chief got wise to this artifice. "Here! Mr. Prime Minister," he said: "You English took my gold. You damn well eat my chocolate."

And suiting his actions to his words, he forthwith seized a chocolate from the ever-present box and held it up to the Prime Minister's mouth. Mr. MacDonald swallowed it with an oath, probably to the effect that all this was beyond the call of duty.

When Queen Salote of the South Seas came to England for the Coronation of Elizabeth II, she attracted much attention. In Salote's kingdom her subjects deny paternity and still hold to an ancient belief that reproduction is achieved by an invasion of spirits from heaven. When a man returns from voyages to other islands after an absence of several years he is not one whit surprised if his wife has family additions. The suspicion would never occur to him that the babies were not his.

Queen Salote was entertained in London by Princess Margaret. At tea the Queen asked the Princess to explain the line of succession to the throne. "What happened to your own succession status, with the arrival of Prince Charles?" asked the inquisitive Queen.

"Well," said the Princess, grinning a little, "actually I became Charley's Aunt."

A witty remark which was probably lost on the Queen, who most probably had not seen the famous comedy of that name.

Turning to Continental royalty, was there ever a Queen so susceptible to stories as was Marie Antoinette? Yet there are very few to be found about her.

Many readers will have visited her toy-box village at Versailles, with its pond and weeping willow, where Her Majesty would imitate the peasantry when the mood struck her. Here at Sans Souci she was surrounded with farmyard animals of all kinds.

One day a visiting friend asked her if her chickens laid eggs, and her reply was devastating: "My chickens do not lay eggs because they don't have to. But if they did they would lay the best eggs in all of France."

Which was the same sort of silly remark as she made when she suggested the starving French peasantry should live on cake, a statement not designed to endear her to the people. Oddly enough, an earlier ruler of France, Louis XIV, was despotic in the fullest sense, but seemingly made the French people like his overbearing tactics.

One of his peasant-citizens went home on a certain evening in a state of reverie. Entering his humble abode he called to his wife: "Guess what happened to me this morning?"

"All right, tell me."

"His Majesty the King spoke to me! Think of that!"

"What did he say?"

"He told me to get out of his way."

At a certain time during his reign, the King became concerned about reports of a gentleman who was said to be the very image of him. Things reached such a point that the man would be mistakenly cheered for being the King as he passed by in his carriage. Report after report reached the King about his double and he finally ordered the man to be brought before him.

Staggered at the resemblance to himself in every way excepting that of age, the King could readily see the reason for the confused identity. Questioning the man, he was surprised to discover that he was of English birth.

"Did your mother ever come to Paris?" asked the King with an air of intense curiosity.

"Yes, often, Sire."

"How old are you?"

"Thirty-six, Sire."

"Tell me," catechized the King. "Did your mother ever come to Paris in such-and-such a year?"

Quickly the young man grasped the subtle innuendo which the King was making and he lost no time in balking it.

"No, Sire," he said with the hint of a smile, "but my father did!"

Despite the much vaunted respectability of British Royalty, adultery is not unknown within its ranks. That profligate monarch King George IV hated his wife Queen Caroline, whose marriage to him he regarded as a matter of State. He continued to live in "sin and unchastity" with his mistress, the beautiful Mrs. Fitzherbert, who was so important to him that she virtually eclipsed the good Queen Caroline. For years the King and his mistress lived together as man and wife, to the distress of the poor Queen.

At the time there was a conundrum going the rounds of London: "What is the difference between Mrs. Fitzherbert and a demi-mondaine?"

The answer was that Mrs. Fitzherbert would break the Seventh Commandment for a sovereign, but not for half-a-crown—a clever play on two sums of money in the British coinage.

Finally King George declared that he intended to divorce his Queen on the grounds of adultery! When the Queen was told the news she smiled wanly: "That's a good one! There's only one man with whom I have ever committed adultery—and that's the husband of Mrs. Fitzherbert!"

Napoleon said: "Every Frenchman has two mistresses, his own and France." Of all French royalty he possessed the finest faculty for retort. To Talleyrand, in whom he recognized immense ability —also a potential traitor—he once said: "Sir, you are in love with yourself. And you don't have a rival on earth!"

When asked why he had created so many orders and medals, he quipped: "Because most men love toys."

No one knew better how to fling an insult. After he had suffered from deception and intrigue at the hands of his tremendous enemy Madame de Staël, he said of her: "She only has one fault. She is insufferable."

And later when her conduct became treasonable, he banished her from Paris and described her as "a piece of dung in a silk stocking." From which epithet Madame de Staël never fully recovered, and gradually sank into contempt.

Nevertheless, Napoleon eventually met his match in verbal sparring when he triumphantly invaded Italy. Brimming with the fruits of victory, he was sitting next to the wife of an Italian official at a large dinner given in his honor.

Napoleon began his conversational overtures brusquely: "Madame, all your countrymen are thieves!"

Naturally, since Napoleon had invaded and looted her country, it seemed to the woman that he was the thief. Yet she could not infer anything so truthful to the Conqueror. Instead she answered by a clever play on words which was also an insinuating shaft. She said: "No Maesta, non tutti, ma buona parte." (No, Sire, not all, but part of them.) The phrase had a subtle connotation for the Emperor's family name and made him turn color.

The nephew of Napoleon the Great was nicknamed Napoleon the Little by his detractor, Victor Hugo. But the title which this Napoleon gave himself was Napoleon III—and since there had been no second Napoleon some of his detractors interpreted the designation as Napoleon!!!

Anyhow, suffice it to say that he loomed large over the European scene and reigned for a number of years—if a little unsteadily. His royal head was likened to a lighting conductor because "so many storms broke over it."

Certainly many people cursed it. Palmerston, the British Prime Minister, who had many dealings with him, referred to his head in more sarcastic terms: "Ideas run in and out of it," he declared, "like rabbits in a warren." And Thomas Carlyle said: "Napoleon's head is like an extinct sulphur pit giving out the smell of rotten eggs."

He was scheduled to marry his cousin the Bonapartist Princess Mathilde, but instead he transferred his affections to Eugénie Montijo who became his Empress (and died in 1920). Princess Mathilde once reflected: "If I had married Louis Napoleon, I would probably have broken open his head to see what, if anything, was inside it."

This unfortunate monarch (he was finally taken prisoner by the Prussians in 1870) was the son of Queen Hortense of Holland who, in the evening of her life, wrote her autobiography. In this book she stated calmly that she had never been involved in an illicit love affair, yet she concluded the royal revelations with an admission of having borne one illegitimate child!

The son was called the Duke of Morny and became one of Napoleon III's ministers in the Second Empire. And he was so proud of his bastardy that he wore a sprig of Hortensia (named after Queen Hortense) in his buttonhole.

This caused the Emperor's immediate family to take umbrage, for it cast aspersions on the Emperor's mother, and Empress Eugénie was allocated to persuade the Duke to refrain from the subtle reference to his bastardy. In a private interview she pointed out that he would receive more favors from the Emperor if he would desist.

The Duke of Morny knew something of the unchaperoned life the Empress had led before she married. She was a famous beauty and her name had been linked in romance with many a notable man. "Are you so prudish, Majesty," he asked, "that you cannot remember one indiscreet liaison?"

The Empress blushed visibly. Somehow she had to squash the subtle innuendo. "I may have had a few love affairs, Monsieur le Duc," she said angrily. "But I assure you, I was still Mademoiselle Montijo until I went to bed with the Emperor."

Eugénie's beauty was not sufficient to hold her husband who took on several mistresses, not the least of whom was the beauteous Contessa de Castiglione. When this lady died, long after her equatorial love affair with Napoleon, she left a request in her will that she be buried in the same nightgown which she had worn on the last occasion she had slept with the Emperor at Compéigne.

Poor Eugénie closed half an eye to her royal husband's infidelities and toyed with anything which could offer amusement. She secretly yearned for the next world, so unhappy was she in this one, and when Daniel Dunglass Home came to France with his amazing demonstration of the Black Arts, she beckoned him to the Tuileries.

This man was an American said to be endowed with supernatural powers. Sessions with him were held at the Tuileries at which he levitated himself so successfully that the Empress was convinced that he could defy the laws of gravity.

Communication with the dead was another of his specialities. At one seance the Empress and her husband sat in a darkened room surrounded by a few privileged courtiers. The amazing Mr. Home was in trance and began droning out messages from the Beyond.

One of these purported to come from Louis XIV, yet another from Napoleon I. Both messages made it clear that the Emperor Napoleon III was not wholly approved of as ruler. At the manifestation of his uncle's spirit, the Emperor started. He got up from his chair as if to receive a benediction. Instead he felt a forcible kick in the rear of his anatomy.

Thiers, one of his worst enemies, noised the story about, adding that the Emperor would never know who kicked him—his uncle or Louis XIV, for both had sufficient reasons in the name of France.

When the final debacle of the Second Empire was approaching, and the Alsace-Lorraine crisis was almost ready to bring about the Franco-Prussian War, a jeweller happened to be at the Tuileries one afternoon discussing with Eugénie the design of a bracelet he was making for her. Napoleon suddenly entered the room and peremptorily dismissed the man. Eugénie intervened: "This is the cleverest jeweller in all France," she said. "He can make a jewel out of anything!"

"Is that so?" said the Emperor sarcastically. And taking a hair from his head, he handed it to the jeweller. "See what you can do with this, and be gone!" he snarled.

The jeweller placed the royal hair carefully into an envelope and left the palace, thoroughly insulted.

A month later the Franco-Prussian War was raging and Napoleon's worries had begun. On the day when things looked blackest, a messenger arrived at the Emperor's headquarters from Paris bringing a small box. Inside the Emperor found the hair he had given the jeweller and attached to each end was a tiny disc of gold. One bore the inscription *Alsace* and the other *Lorraine*. And written on the card accompanying the gift was: "You hold them by a hair!" In a few weeks both districts were in enemy hands.

Even the son of this ill-starred sovereign met with a tragic fate. He was killed by a Zulu assegai in Africa when on a reconnoitering expedition with the British Army in 1879. Disraeli remarked at the time: "The Zulus not only defeated our generals, but they settled the fate of a French dynasty as well."

The dynasty of King Zog of Albania was settled by Benito Mussolini, but this jovial monarch had a good time while it lasted. He married an attractive American woman and some years ago brought to the United States his three uncomely sisters with a view to finding them wealthy husbands—a project in which he failed.

A good story is told by an English diplomat who visited King Zog's palace in the Balkans. In the midst of a banquet he suddenly missed his watch, and since it represented considerable value to him, he spoke to the King about his loss. His Majesty said nothing but got up from his place and went over to speak to one of his ministers who was seated at the end of the table. And then, as if by magic, he returned with the missing watch.

"Your Majesty, how did you do it? Where on earth . . ."

Zog put a hushing finger to his lips. "Say nothing," he snickered, "I found it on the Minister for the Interior and he probably hasn't noticed I sneaked it off him."

Royalty has never been too popular in Ireland, although the Irish people understand thoroughly the scriptural precept for kingship. During the Battle of the Boyne, King William II was retreating with his Irish army after a serious defeat by William of Orange.

Lady Tyrconnel, a loyal Irishwoman and the wife of one of William's adjutants, met the retreating monarch upon his arrival in Dublin. "Lady Tyrconnel!" the King said angrily, "your countrymen ran away. They ran basely!"

"Yes," replied the Irishwoman, "and I notice that Your Majesty has won the race."

No doubt the sarcasm was wasted on him, but he got out of Ireland posthaste. Significantly, the Irish had Kings and Queens of their own in the faraway days, and by far the most interesting was the famous Pirate Queen, Grace O'Malley of County Mayo. She was as famous for her maritime forays as for her husbands and the way she would rid herself of them upon occasion. This fascinating Queen had more husbands than history has been able to count, and she always stipulated that at the end of a year she could end her union with any of them by the statement: "I dismiss you." She severed herself from at least ten men by this simple device.

The powerful Queen Elizabeth requested an interview with her in England for the purpose of coming to an arrangement about English shipping which Queen Grace had been raiding with monotonous regularity. When they met, Grace made it clear to Elizabeth that she was addressing a sister-Queen and required mutual respect. She shook Queen Elizabeth's hand manishly when it was held out for her to kiss. "Cousin," she said regally, "if you wish me to leave your ships alone, I will allow you to make my son a Lord."

And Queen Elizabeth was so amused by this wild Irishwoman that she created her son the first Earl of Mayo, a title existing to this day. Queen Grace and her son parted company after a quarrel, and the Earl fled to England where he took up residence in the placid countryside. Elizabeth heard that he was in her country and paid a call upon him at his modest abode. "My Lord," said the Queen, "what a small house you have!"

"Ah, Majesty," replied Mayo, "my house is adequate. It is you who has made me too big for my house!"

Queen Elizabeth II makes an appearance now and then in Northern Ireland where extensive precautions have to be taken each time to preserve her safety. The Republic of Ireland is never enthusiastic about these visits because it feels that the royal visit compromises Irish sovereignty. Last time one of the Dublin dailies commented: "The Northern Irish gave the Queen a good reception upon her departure."

Interestingly enough the Queen is not accepted as Elizabeth II in Scotland. The Scotch insist that Her Majesty is the first Sovereign of the United Kingdom to bear the name of Elizabeth. In designating herself the second Elizabeth, the Scots say she is presupposing that Elizabeth Tudor was Queen of Scotland which she never was, although she did execute Mary, Queen of all the Scots!

... 8

Legal Laughs

At the end of the last century there was a flourishing firm of lawyers in New York named Ketcham and Cheetham. Oddly enough, the first names of the partners were Isaac and Uriah, so they could have headed their company I. Ketcham and U. Cheetham! Even in the present time there is a noted firm of lawyers in a midwestern City owning the delicious combination of Dilly, Daly and Dolittle.

Other gems of nomenclature taken at random are worth adding. I find in the current Manhattan telephone directory the name of Wind and Wind, and in the city of Port Clinton, Ohio, I am told there is a partnership entitled Stahl, Stahl and Stahl.

Doubtless all of them are reputable, as was the distinguished lawyer of a few generations ago who called himself Abel Crooke —and that was his name! He it was who had a sharp exchange of words with the great criminal lawyer Max Steuer, who was known to every crook within a radius of a thousand miles of New York.

It seems that Mr. Crooke was doing very nicely defending the gangsters of his day until Max Steuer came along and bestrode the legal scene with his eloquence and masterly handling of the juror's psychology. "You make me sick," said Crooke in court one day to Steuer, "with your three B's—blarney, bluff and bluster."

"Ah," Max Steuer said, as a gleam of satisfaction came over his face. "But you never complained about my 'bees' until they began sucking your honey!"

Another American lawyer for the defense was Clarence Darrow. One day in court he was dealing with a difficult witness. The man had a vinous complexion and Darrow thought it a good line to take that the witness might be considered a drunkard.

"Do you drink?" asked Darrow.

"That's my business," answered the witness angrily.

"And do you have any other?" jeered Darrow triumphantly.

In the Scopes Trial, which brought Darrow to the height of his fame, everyone was stifled by the southern heat as well as by the searing sarcasm of Darrow and William Jennings Bryan. Scopes sat on the witness chair bathed in perspiration all one day. Limply he left the courtroom with Darrow who cooled him off with this remark: "If the jury would only mistake your perspiration for inspiration, I'd get you an acquittal."

In the Leopold and Loeb case, Darrow scored against a witness for the prosecution. The man had contradicted himself several times and Darrow had cast aspersions on his veracity. "I am wedded to the truth, Mr. Darrow," he said pompously.

"And how long have you been a widower?" posed Darrow.

One thing which Darrow was forced to play down in this trial was the excellent education and scholarship of Nathan Leopold. It did not help the defense for the jury to know that Leopold was one of the outstanding ornithologists in America, especially as the plea of the murderer was one of insanity. Bird experts are usually the sanest of men!

In jail Leopold continued his studies in this field and still paid his dues to the American Ornithological Society in which he held high rank. He happened to enter a newspaper competition for birdwatchers, which he won. Ironically his prize was a trip around the world!

Judge Joseph E. Gary of the Superior Court in Chicago was a man who equalled Darrow's humor. His sardonic wit was well displayed when once a juror was trying to be excused on the grounds of illness. "What's the matter with you?" Judge Gary asked.

"I have an unpleasant disease, Your Honor."

"What sort of disease?" demanded the Judge.

"The itch, Your Honor."

Judge Gary smiled slyly at the clerk. "Scratch him," he said.

Lots of good stories cluster round the personality of Justice Oliver Wendell Holmes. One day he was in conversation with a Judge who was suspected of selling justice. Holmes made some rather inferential remarks to him about the unpleasant rumors regarding his reputation. "I'll have you know I'm not for sale, Mr. Holmes," the Judge said fiercely.

"Probably not," said Justice Holmes, "but you've been in the shop window a long time."

This recalls a begging letter received by Justice Holmes from a woman whom he hardly knew. She said: "I would like to ask you for the loan of ten dollars just for the sake of old friendship." To which request Holmes paid no attention. Later, however, the woman wrote to him again: "If I do not get the loan of ten dollars from you, I'm ruined."

This time Holmes replied. He wrote, "Madame: If a woman can be ruined for ten dollars, she is not worth saving."

A good story is told about a case in which he sentenced a notorious criminal to a long term of imprisonment. He made some scathing remarks about some of the man's accomplices, who could not be convicted due to lack of evidence.

Some days later one of these men is supposed to have held up the Justice at the point of a gun. "Take back what you said about me or I'll fire!"

"Fire away!" said the fearless Holmes, "I'm not afraid. You couldn't hit the mark the way I did!"

Abraham Lincoln had a distinctive line of legal wit which he used to advantage at the bar, and always charmingly. Describing his opponent in a case whose conduct at the bar was erratic, Lincoln said: "The moment my learned opponent begins to talk, his mental processes cease. He is like a little steamboat which I once saw on the Saugamon River. The little steamer had a five-foot boiler and a seven-foot whistle, and every time it whistled the engine stopped—like my opponent's mind."

Another tale is told about the time Lincoln was legally embattled with a disreputable lawyer. Oddly enough, the lawyer challenged a juror because of being personally acquainted with Lincoln. So Abe began challenging several other jurors on the grounds that they might know his legal adversary.

Judge Davis was presiding and interrupted: "Mr. Lincoln," he said, "just because a juror may know either of you, it does not disqualify him."

"Oh, I'm quite aware of that, Your Honor," said Lincoln. "What worries me is that some of the jury may *not* know my adversary, and that would place me at a disadvantage."

Interplay of wit between criminal and judge is still common in England. As far back as Tudor times there are records of this strange type of humor. In the reign of good Queen Bess there was never a harder-hearted judge than Sir Nicholas Bacon. Once he was about to sentence a man named Hogg who was begging for clemency. As soon as the Judge put on his head the black cap which signified hanging for the criminal, there was a yell from him: "Your Lordship! Please have mercy. My name is Hogg, and yours Bacon! Surely we should not be separated in this way?"

The Judge fixed his granite jaw: "I fear we cannot be considered kindred in this instance," he said. "You are forgetting that hog is not bacon until well hanged!"

The opposite of Judge Bacon was Judge Henry Gildersleeve, known affectionately as "Gildy" to his friends, who presided some time ago over the Criminal Courts of New York. On the subject of the death sentence he once declared: "I never sentence a man to death. God does that. I only arrange the date."

There is a story told about the court of this lovable man that one particular miscreant came before it periodically, usually in the late autumn, so that he could spend the winters in jail. Judge Gildersleeve would oblige with a six months' term for such offense as petty theft, etc.

But once the man came before him accused of wrong-doing which could not draw such a long sentence. "This time you go to prison for three months," said Gildersleeve.

The man's face turned color. "Please send me to jail for six months, Your Honor," he cried. And he continued to make such a noise that Judge Gildersleeve felt constrained to say: "If you go on like that I won't send you to prison at all!"

By contrast there is an amusing instance which took place in the Old Bailey Court of Lord Justice Hewart. He had sentenced a man to a long term of imprisonment. The man put up a hue and cry: "You can see for yourself that I am old and never can live to serve this long sentence, Your Lordship."

"Then serve as much of it as you can," said the Judge.

Before he became Lord Chief Justice of England, Lord Hewart was attached to the Assizes of Manchester. Before him one day was a man accused of pickpocketing. Lord Hewart heard the evidence which was very condemning, and he was surprised when the man asked for a lawyer to defend him. "You were caught with your hand inside a man's pocket. What can a lawyer say in your defense?" he asked.

There was a pause and then the man said: "That's what I'm anxious to know."

Interplay of wit between lawyer and judge is rarer, but anything likely to mitigate the tedium of legal proceedings in court is acceptable to all concerned. Judge Brandeis gave a snappy reply to a long-winded lawyer who asked him for latitude: "I don't mind your latitude," he said to the lawyer. "What I object to is your longitude."

Perhaps the drollest figure in the annals of American law was

Judge Ben Lindsay, of "companionate marriage" fame. Among many projects, he ran what might be called a marriage repair shop, a court where people without means could go and argue the matter of whether to divorce or not.

One day a rather vague type of housewife came to see him, asking the Judge's advice. She had a grudge against her husband, but it was difficult for her to state it. Judge Lindsay questioned her: "Does your husband ill-treat you?"

"No, he is the kindliest of men."

"Does he ever fail to support you?"

"No, he has been most generous."

"Well," said Judge Lindsay, "will you please tell the Court just what your grievance is."

The lady was wrapped in thought for a minute or two. "You see, sir," she said disarmingly, "there's a certain amount of doubt whether my husband is the father of my fourth child."

Another story ascribed to Judge Lindsay is about a woman who had worked for him and his wife as a servant for some years and came one day asking that the Judge might recommend her son for a job.

"Why, Maggie," said Judge Lindsay, "I had no idea you were married. You have never mentioned this lad of yours before."

"Well," the woman said, "I'm not married, that's true. But I haven't been entirely neglected."

The wit of Judge Lindsay is demonstrated in a breeze he had with a lawyer in court one day. It was a case questioning the validity of a divorce decison in another state. There was a sharp altercation which Judge Lindsay resented.

Later the Judge ruled that the divorce could be granted in his state under laws pertaining to incompatibility of temperament.

"May I submit to Your Honor that the disagreement between us earlier could have led to a divorce between us?"

"There you are wrong," said Judge Lindsay, smiling broadly. "That would have been merely a judicial separation."

The saying "Judge not that ye be not judged" is commonly taken for a divine command, but it is also a statement in fact. During the claim by Nell Gwynn for support by the State after she had lost her royal lover, there was a reference to the lady's past history. The judge asked her in his most judicial tone: "Under whose protection are you now, Madam?"

Nell tossed a smile at him as sweetly as she might have done with one of her famous oranges: "Under yours, I hope, my Lord."

Because her King had made no provision for her in his will, she was left to the mercy of a tragic fate. In Ireland, the most frequent type of case in common law is against wills. Daniel O'Connell was once representing a client whose legacy was being impugned by the existence of a later will suspected of being forged. The great Irish advocate was attacking the plaintiff violently with every verbal thrust he could muster.

"So you insist that the testator was alive when he made this will?"

"Indeed he was. There was much life in him."

Then O'Connell fired a shaft which brought down the house with laughter. "You mean he had a fly in his mouth!" He won his case.

A second instance of this great man's wit may be cited. During the proceedings of a court in a country town with the windows of the building wide open, O'Connell was addressing the judge. Outside in an adjoining field a donkey brayed loudly. The judge intervened humorously: "One at a time, Mr. O'Connell."

Later, when the judge was delivering his instructions to the jury, the donkey was heard to bray again, even louder. O'Connell rose from his chair and said: "I am sorry, My Lord, but there seems to be such an echo that I can scarcely make out what Your Lordship is saying."

Many amusing passages of arms are recorded about Tim Healy, an Irishman of blessed memory and possessor of a barbed and brilliant wit. When pleading the cause of his client in a certain case, the opposing counsel, a man of callous reputation, was moved to tears.

Rising to reply, Healy made history with a very precious piece of repartee. He said: "What we have just witnessed in this Court must be regarded as the most remarkable flow of water since Moses struck the rock."

And in another case, when Healy was practicing at the English bar, he scored again. His adversary had produced a witness whose testimony was damaging to the case for his client. Healy was in possession of facts about the witness which showed that she was a woman of loose morals, and therefore he cast aspersions of this nature upon her.

The opposing counsel was outraged. "I'll have you know that my client is as white as the driven snow."

"Oh, I see," said Healy calmly. "A hoar frost."

The name of Timothy Healy will live as much for his witticisms as for his loyalty to Ireland, which country he once described as "an ethereal young lady with her heart full of sun and her head flowering with wit." During "the trouble" there was no doubt on which side Healy was. On the eve of a rebel's execution to take place at Kilmainham Gaol (where many an Irishman lies today under quicklime), he produced a letter in court (from the prison doctor who was secretly on the Irish side) which read: "Paddy O'Sullivan is ill and cannot be removed from his cell without grave risk to his life."

The Irish gaze with a look of drollery even into the eyes of death. In a double hanging at Mountjoy Prison, Dublin, two men were to be hanged for the same murder. They were permitted to toss up to decide which man was to go to the gallows first. The loser said: "Jack, do you mind holding my hat for a minute?"

In the same vein there is the story of the two murderers about to be hanged at San Quentin Prison in California. One was from Los Angeles and the other from San Francisco. Equally proud of their native cities, they had quarrelled about the merits of the two domiciles. In their final farewell, one said to the other: "Los Angeles is lousy!" And the other man hissed back: "San Francisco is the dregs of the world."

Instances of judges insulting each other are not unknown. A pompous judge was Lord Skully, who kept his colleagues at arm's length. Just the opposite was his contemporary Lord Monck, a convivial member of the bench if ever there was one. Once he decided to try to get a rise out of Lord Monck, but he only did it once. "Well, Skull, old chap," he greeted him. "That's my nick-name for you!"

Lord Skully stopped in his tracks and exalted himself: "If you omit the Y in my name," he said tartly, "why not add it to your own and make yourself a monkey?"

As a matter of fact, one of the most amusing cases in recent English law annals was one involving a monkey and took place in the halcyon days prior to World War II. The animal had been peremptorily sentenced to death by a magistrate for biting his human cousins, and animal-lovers all over England had raised a violent protest.

No less an advocate than Sir Henry Curtis-Bennett was re-tained to defend the monkey (which he did largely because his own children had begged him).

Being a very astute lawyer (many living criminals owe their lives to his forensic ability), he was fully aware that if he dared to take the animal into court unmuzzled, and the animal behaved, the case would be won.

So Sir Henry did take the animal into court, carrying it in his arms. As witness after witness testified to the monkey's savagery, it behaved with absolute propriety. The verdict was "Not Guilty," and triumphantly Sir Henry took the creature in his arms, patted it on the head, and walked into the outside world to the clicking of newspaper cameras.

Suddenly the animal became temperamental. As Sir Henry was

about to enter a waiting motor car, it bit him on the hand. A sarcastic journalist asked: "Was it possible that the monkey knew he could not be tried twice for the same offense?"

The fact remains that few people make good winesses and every lawyer knows what Curtis-Bennett knew in the case of the monkey: that every man on trial can convict himself by his conduct on the witness stand. When Colonel Dreyfus was being tried for treason in France, Labori, his eminent counsel, did not want his client to go on the stand. "I knew Dreyfus was innocent of treason," he said afterwards. "My chief concern was that he might admit to something worse."

Justice itself is always a matter of degree. In certain parts of Africa, they handle the "in-law" problem in summary fashion. The father- and mother-in-law of a certain age are hoisted up a tall tree which is then shaken furiously. If the couple manage to remain atop, it is considered a good omen. They are allowed to live!

Only a few years ago the Ranee of Sarawak wrote a series of articles about her country. She insisted that the State of Sarawak was free of crime. And yet she wound up her first article: "Next week I shall tell you about one of my subjects who came to me with the head of her rival under her arm, asking my advice as to the next move she should make to get the man she coveted."

All the same, jungle justice is equitable. One of the finest legal decisions was made by Paul Kruger, President of the Boer Republic. Two natives came to him when he was making a tour in an uncivilized part of the country. The men were quarrelling about a parcel of land left them by their father, the Chief of the tribe. They could not agree on a division and the eldest wanted the whole of it.

Kruger laid down a fine dictum. He said: "One of you must draw a line through the property, making sure it divides it equally. And the other of you must make the choice which piece to take!"

Which sounds like the sublime sort of wisdom one associates with Daniel Webster, who, incidentally, could appreciate a joke as fully as anyone. One that he told with relish was about a friend of his who was defending a gambler charged with murder. There was some doubt if the man was guilty of manslaughter or murder, however, and his lawyer put up a superb plea in his behalf.

The gambler's friends were rich and decided to nudge the ways of Justice. They found a weak juror who agreed to hold out for a "Not Guilty" verdict in consideration of five thousand dollars.

After this verdict was achieved and the juror was paid off, the gambler happened to meet another member of the jury. He was naturally curious to know how much resistance there had been to his acquittal. "Resistance?" asked the man. "The only resistance was by So-and-So," and he named the bribed juror. "He held out six hours for making you guilty and we had to bring him round."

Some very strange last wills and testaments have been recorded. The following was filed for probate in the estate of a thoroughly disabused millionaire: "To my wife I leave her lover and the knowledge for her that I was not the fool she thought I was. [There followed a bequest of a trust fund.]

"To my daughter I leave one hundred thousand dollars to prove to her husband that his marriage to her was the best deal he ever accomplished.

"To my partner in business I leave the advice that he had better take into the firm some very clever man to replace me, or he will go bankrupt.

"To my chauffeur I leave all my motor cars. He almost ruined them, and now he can finish the job."

... 9

Political Polemics

When Senator Taft was barnstorming for the Presidency he drew one of the loudest bursts of applause in the history of campaigning. He was speaking to a noisy meeting in Detroit, doing his best to make his point. From the middle of the audience, a virago of a woman shouted: "You're terrible. If you were my husband, I'd poison you!"

There was a hush throughout the audience as the insult was absorbed. Unabashed, Taft yelled back in the same vein: "Madam, if I were married to you, I'd *take* poison!" For that excellent squelch he was cheered and applauded to the echo.

A similar thing happened to President Theodore Roosevelt. He was campaigning somewhere in the Midwest and a lady heckler became annoyed with him because he paid no attention to her remonstrations, which she kept repeating loudly and rudely.

Finally she flung at him in the most strident voice, so all could hear: "I don't like your politics or your moustache!"

Roosevelt assumed his favorite attitude, right hand holding the lapel of his coat and the other adjusting his spectacles. "Don't distress yourself, Madam. You are unlikely to come into touch with either." The crowd roared their approval, and Roosevelt continued uninterrupted further.

No one ever accused Roosevelt of lacking the courage of his

convictions. He was transparently honest and, being a fine conversationalist, was sometimes indiscreet. Once he appeared at a public gathering with a bandaged hand. Someone asked: "What's the matter with the President's hand?"

And the friend, who knew him well enough to be facetious, replied: "Oh, Teddy's probably been trying to hold his tongue."

Teddy Roosevelt was not in office at the time of the German sinking of the "Lusitania." The disaster made the public all the more angry because the German Ambassador had announced that the ship was going to be sunk, and he had warned Americans not to travel on her.

In the course of a conversation within his own coterie, Roosevelt commented: "Had I been in power, the 'Lusitania' would still be afloat! I would have put the German Ambassador and his entire staff aboard on the threatened voyage and then sent them packing back to Germany."

Teddy Roosevelt wrote all his own speeches himself, and was also an able authority on history, as his essays prove. In recent times it has become the practice for Presidents to have their speeches written for them by special henchmen. Doubtless this is due to the greater demands upon the energy of the man in office than heretofore.

It is generally known that Robert E. Sherwood wrote a great many speeches for President Franklin D. Roosevelt. In one of these, it is said, the President took exception to just one word. But Sherwood was adamant. He thought it had a good deal of connotation.

"Please keep it in. I think the word important."

Said F.D.R., "So use it in my next speech!"

Some people may link the name of Franklin Roosevelt with heightened taxation, overlooking the genuine vision which he possessed. The following stories could not offend his warmest admirers nor thrill his detractors.

Two ardent Republicans were having their child christened

before the war. In the church the father was holding the baby in front of the baptismal font. When asked the Christian name of the child, he gave the name of Roosevelt.

His wife, an anti-Rooseveltian, looked askant. After the ceremony she said: "Why in the name of God did you call him after that man? You know how I dislike the sound of his name."

"Well," replied the husband, "I just couldn't resist it. As I held our child in our arms, he started smiling at me. And in a little while he was soaking me."

The next story is more whimsical. Everyone remembers the controversial lend-lease, so offensive to certain sections of the American public. President Roosevelt was vilified by some, and praised extravagantly by others, for initiating aid to England. Anyway, here is a story invented by someone in the former category:

The souls of Roosevelt and Churchill fly up to heaven. With true British pertinacity, Churchill arrives ahead of F.D.R. To his surprise he finds the Golden Gates closed and no sign of St. Peter nearby. He cries alarmed to F.D.R. who is not far behind:

"Franklin! The gates are closed!"

"Don't worry, Winston," cried F.D.R. "All you have to do is to break them down. I'll pay for them."

In England the bane of the capitalist and hereditary classes used to be David Lloyd George. One might say that the "Welsh Wizard" anticipated Roosevelt's program for social welfare which began pyramiding taxation in both countries.

In any case, Lloyd George imposed taxation on the rich as painlessly as possible. He possessed the gift of double talk to such a degree it was said of him he could make the dullest subject fascinating. Winston Churchill admired him always, and once said: "If Lloyd George was ever forced to jump out of an aeroplane at a great height, he would not only fall on his feet, but would discover many interesting things on the way down."

Lloyd George taxed the rich but also prided himself on keeping a few millionaires among his coterie of friends. So when Ernest Shackleton, the polar explorer, came to him asking to be introduced to someone who might finance his next expedition, Lloyd George proudly introduced him to the richest of his friends.

A few days later Lloyd George met Shackleton and asked him how he had fared.

"Very well indeed," said the great explorer. "Your friend was charming and considerate to me."

"Tell me more," said Lloyd George, pleased.

"Well," continued Shackleton, "he offered me ten thousand pounds for my expenses, provided I would take you along with me to the Pole. And he promised me one million pounds if I were to leave you there by mistake."

In the course of negotiations with Lloyd George during the Irish Trouble, Mr. De Valera doubtless wished him further. Several sharp exchanges of words are on record between these two great men.

Lloyd George once called "Dev" "the Spanish onion in the Irish stew." To which "Dev" replied: "Mr. Lloyd George is conveniently elsewhere when it comes to the rights of the Irish nation. He is the incarnation of the British Empire, which was created in a moment of world absent-mindedness."

The British Prime Minister made another gibe: "Mr. De Valera is so slippery to deal with," he said, "it is like trying to pick up a piece of quicksilver with a fork."

And "Dev" fired back: "Trying to argue with Lloyd George is like going for a walk with a grasshopper."

As the world knows, Lloyd George was only temporarily successful in quashing Irish resistance in 1916 (which year is similar in Irish history to 1776 in American). The name of Lloyd George was anathema to the Irish ever afterwards. When he lost his election and was removed from the political scene forever, a Dublin daily commented:

"Mr. Lloyd George has been for years pretty generally despised abroad. He is now equally distinguished at home."

The Welsh Wizard was never at a loss for words. Once when campaigning in an attempt to come back politically he began his speech with:

"I am here . . . ," then paused to collect his thoughts. He reiterated: "I am here . . . ," and a vulgar voice from the crowd yelled: "So am I!"

Lloyd George narrowed his basilisk eyes and flung an angry look in the direction of the heckler.

"Yes," he said calmly, "but there is a difference. I am *all* here!" And thereafter the audience was his.

One of his political opponents was Sir John Simon (later Lord Simon), the great statesman and legal genius. Someone said to him one day: "You'd better look out. Lloyd George is going to stage a comeback. I have heard he has been having monkey gland treatment in order to give him the energy."

"I don't think I have to worry," smiled Sir John, shrewdly. "They'll never make an old monkey into a new one."

Odd things have happened in Irish politics. There was the time when the head of the I.R.A., that most war-like of organizations, sought refuge in the offices of a pacifist society! For seven hundred years the Irish have fought the English only to be plunged into peace when a perfectly good war came along in 1939.

Of course the political implications of Irish neutrality were enormous. Angry accusations were made by the Allied representatives in Dublin that it was the center for international espionage. This was vehemently denied by the Irish Government authorities, and in the light of statistics it is now known that there were surprisingly few spies in the country during Hitler's War— the most notable being the German Minister who was accused by his ally, the Italian Minister, of following him!

The best story about Ireland and the war was about the two
Irishmen in the R.A.F. who were bombing Berlin. With the
flak flying all around them and the anti-aircraft doing its worst,
one of the men says: "Thank God De Valera kept us out of war!"

A very amusing situation arose in the matter of a shipment of
oranges to England from Jaffa which caused an "international"
incident between the British and Irish Governments during the
war. The much-needed oranges arrived off the English coast in
the midst of enemy bombing. Since the docks of Liverpool had
been so badly damaged that unloading the oranges might be a
matter of weeks, the Minister of Food feared that they might go
bad and offered them to the Government of Eire.

The offer was accepted with alacrity, but in the meantime
Winston Churchill heard of it and ordered that the oranges be
transhipped to another English port. The fruit had not been un-
loaded at Dublin, whose authorities protested in vain that the
precious cargo was theirs.

Upon the final landing of it in England, the Irish Government
lodged a note of protest with the English Minister of Food who
appealed for instructions to Mr. Churchill. The Prime Minister
wrote a memo: "Just tell De Valera," the note ran, "that he
doesn't deserve any oranges. We'll send him some raspberries
instead!"

In Dublin they tell a spurious story about Winston Churchill's
visit to Stalin at Yalta. (When the Irish don't like someone, they
invent stories about them!) Churchill and Stalin were spending
an evening together, matching each other drink for drink of
vodka. During a lively line of conversation, Churchill said more
than he ought about the Russian ideology. So scathing was he
about Communism that the Marshal brought the meeting to an
abrupt close and said a cold good night.

Next morning, Churchill awoke with a terrific headache and
with only a vague memory of what had happened. Gradually it
dawned upon him that he owed Stalin an apology for the things

he had said about the Russian way of life. He reminded himself that a gentleman must put himself in the wrong in social matters, so he instructed his secretary to call upon the secretary of the Marshal and tender an apology.

This done, Churchill's messenger was about to leave the Kremlin when the Communist official called him back. He said: "You know, actually Mr. Churchill didn't have to worry. You see the only other person who overheard the conversation between him and the Marshal was the interpreter—*and he's dead.*"

Not many people have scored against Winston Churchill. Stories abound to prove his command of any situation. Politics not only makes strange bedfellows, but as Churchill himself must be aware, it makes fellows strange. Who could have foreseen that General Smuts, Prime Minister of South Africa, once the avowed enemy of England and the persecutor of Winston Churchill, should live to call him "an incomparable man." Was it not Smuts who had published a notice throughout the Boer territory of South Africa which read: "WANTED! Dead or alive! Winston Churchill. 25 years old. 5 feet eight inches tall. Indifferent build. Walks with a bend forward. Pale complexion. Red-brownish hair. Small toothbrush moustache. Talks through nose and cannot pronounce the letter S properly."

Churchill has had more adventures than Buffalo Bill, not the least of which was his escape from his captors in the Boer War, which occasioned this search for him.

He has said of himself: "I look like all babies and all babies look like me." Which brings to mind the remark of Lord Charles Beresford, likening him to an infant. At this time Lord Charles was M.P. for East Woolwich and Churchill was at the very outset of his political career. He made a rather sweeping statement in the House of Commons on the *status quo* of the Navy which annoyed the Lord Charles.

"I think I know more on this subject than this precocious young man," sneered Lord Charles, "for I was in command of one of

His Majesty's ships when he was doing his best at the business end of a feeding bottle."

Churchill bided his time for a retaliation. In another encounter with Lord Charles he replied with the following: "When my Right Honorable friend rose to his feet a few minutes ago, he had not the least idea of what he was going to say. Moreover, he did not know what he was saying when speaking. And when he sat down, he was doubtless unable to remember what he had said!"

Some months later the atmosphere of the House of Commons was charged with electricity when Lord Charles Beresford and Winston Churchill again went for each other. Lord Charles was still smarting over the last squelch he had suffered and was determined to clip the wings of the youthful Churchill, who had attacked another Navy policy.

"I suggest," he began, "that Winston Churchill is suffering from beri-beri, the cardinal symptom of which is a swollen head."

Here Churchill was quick to exhibit his knowledge of medicine:

"My Right Honorable friend is wrong. The disease of which he speaks has for its chief symptom swollen feet!"

The witticism was a good one, but it laid Churchill open to a nasty retort. Lord Charles was quick to use it:

"That's even better!" he chirped. "What I mean to imply is that you are too big for your boots!"

Not much love has been lost between Lady Astor and Winston Churchill. Once, when tilting with him in a private conversation about the position of women in politics she asked him testily:

"What is the difference between you and me?"

And the great leader gave a good example of his devastating wit:

"I can't conceive, Madame!"

That particular story may or may not be true, but it *is* a fact that the famed American-born Member of Parliament scored nicely against Churchill. She was debating in the House of

Commons about farming and Churchill, anxious to proceed with another issue, said:

"I venture to say that my Right Honorable friend, so redolent of other knowledge, knows nothing about farming. I'll even make a bet that she doesn't know how many toes a pig has!"

"Oh, yes I do!" quipped the irrepressible Lady Astor. "Take off your little shoosies and have a look!"

As regards Churchillian wit and riposte, a long time before Hitler's shadow cast itself so menacingly over the world, he was asked what he thought of the Nazi leader: "No one can have a higher opinion of him that I do," said Churchill. "I think he's a dirty little guttersnipe."

Culling at random from the many anecdotes told about Sir Winston (why did he have to take that title? He was such a colossal Mister!), someone is said to have asked him about the illness of Ernest Bevin which was something of a mystery. Bevin was Churchill's political foe, but personal friend. "They tell me," Churchill said, with tongue in cheek, "that the Foreign Secretary is suffering from a thrombosis, which, in his case, is a clot on the Constitution."

Another quip at the expense of the Labor Party was made as he passed by Sir Stafford Cripps (a rather pontifical man and often a thorn in Churchill's side): "There but for the grace of God goes God."

At a meeting of the Coalition Cabinet, one of the Labor Ministers was absent. A message came through that he would not be able to attend due to illness. "Nothing trivial, I hope?" said Churchill in his kindliest tone.

The Churchill "crisis" mind is the envy of all who know him. He can face the starkest terrors and seemingly not turn one of the few hairs he has left. During one of the worst German air raids upon London, he asked for an opportunity to see the bombs falling from a good vantage point.

A certain section of London was ablaze. Nothing would stop Churchill from going to the roof of Ten Downing Street for sight of the scene.

As he sat transfixed with a few of his staff standing nearby, a servant came up to the roof to announce that the house was filled with smoke. Something was blocking the chimney, and Lady Churchill was nearly suffocating with the fumes.

It was then discovered that Churchill was sitting on the chimney vent. As soon as he removed himself from his contrived seat the smoke began puffing freely once again.

Only recently he was staying with some friends who own one of the famous baronial halls of England. There he was given a room containing a bed said to have been slept in by the great Duke of Wellington. When asked next morning how he had slumbered, Sir Winston replied: "I now know why the fine old soldier was called 'The Iron Duke.'"

Incidentally, the Duke of Wellington was very touchy about having been born in Ireland. (Churchill just missed being born there, too, since his mother was in Dublin a few days before his birth.) When a newspaper called the Duke an Irishman, the old man saw red. "If a man is born in a stable, does it make him a horse?" was his irascible protest.

Harking back to De Valera, who used to be the most polemical personality in politics (he is, by the way, no longer anti-English), it will be remembered that he was arrested by the British in 1916 for sedition. The great Irish leader was actually seized while he was making a speech in his constituency. Taken into custody, he was transported to England and there court-martialed. Awarded the supreme penalty of death, this was commuted to life imprisonment on account of his American birth.

Fortunately for Ireland, he managed to escape from Lincoln Prison, where he was serving his time, and made his way to America. Two years later, he was back in the Emerald Isle leading the fight for freedom again. One of his first appearances happened to be in County Clare, his constituency, where he had been seized by the British constabulary. Mr. De Valera began his address with: "As I was saying when I was so rudely interrupted two years ago . . . "

For some reason, De Valera has been awarded the reputation for never laughing. Actually I can vouch for the fact that he has a delicious sense of humor. During a long friendship, I have seen him laugh often—and when he laughs he can look astonishingly young. On one of my visits to him at the Dail (Irish Parliament), I found the Taoiseach (Prime Minister) in fine fettle. The statue of Queen Victoria had just been removed from outside his window—a great mountain of stone which had no further *raison d'être* after the proclamation of the Republic.

I asked Mr. De Valera what he thought of the removal and he smiled wryly: "You will be surprised to know that I felt she should be left where she was. Her Majesty was covered with verdigris! The Irish climate had turned her almost completely green!"

Known as "the Uncrowned King of Ireland," De Valera's life strangely resembles that of Abraham Lincoln, and there is more than a suggestion of a physical comparison between the two men. Like Lincoln, De Valera was forced to plunge his country into a civil war, and the early life of the Irish leader was spent doing manual labor on a farm. When he dies, is it not likely that the same phrase might be applied to his passing as was used about the American Liberator?—"Like the fall of a mighty oak in a forest, his passing leaves a vast void against the sky."

Lincoln suffered the "slings and arrows of outrageous fortune" to the full. Stanton called Lincoln an unpleasant name during one of their fiercely fought campaigns for the Presidency and even went so far as to say that explorers were fools to go to Africa in search of apes, when they could find the perfect type in Springfield, Illinois.

Lincoln, in all his humility, never hit back at Stanton even when it would have been simple to do so. Some years later, however, when tempers were not running so high, Stanton paid a call at the White House. The President was indisposed with a chill.

When informed of the visit by Mrs. Lincoln, he said, "If he calls at a later date, let me know. If I am alive, I shall be delighted to see him. If I am not alive, he will doubtless be pleased to see me."

Once Lincoln was openly insulted by a drunken man in the auditorium where he was speaking. "Did I have to pay a dollar to see the ugliest man in the whole of the U.S.A.?" he shouted.

There were cries of "throw him out," but Lincoln quelled them. Thrusting his head into the crowd from the vantage point of the platform, and shading his eyes with his hand, he shouted back: "Yes, Sir, I am afraid that you were charged a dollar for that privilege. But I have it for nothing. Thank you."

In those days it seems that personal remarks in politics were the vogue. Senator A. H. Stephens came in for a few of them because he was the smallest Senator of his times. But his mental stature was great, as will be seen by his wonderful wit.

In a Congressional debate, he was faced with a furious opponent, a Senator known for his abusive tirades. "You little know-nothing," the Senator shouted to Stephens, "I could swallow you whole and never know that I had eaten anything."

"In that case," murmured Stephens, "you would have more brains in your belly than ever you had in your head."

In another tiff with the same Senator, Stephens called out: "My opponent is not fit to carry swill to swine . . ."

There came cries of "Order! Order!" And Stephens was told to apologize.

"Mr. Speaker," said Stephens meekly, "I do apologize. The Senator is absolutely fit for the duty to which I referred."

Congressman Reed is another figure who ranks in anecdotal Americana. To the famous and rather prudish statement attributed to Henry Clay: "I would rather be right than President," Reed said: "He doesn't have to worry. He'll never be either."

Naturally this was repeated, and Clay did not allow it to pass unnoticed. Some time later the two men were engaged in a prolonged conversation. Shaking Reed firmly by the hand, Clay said: "Come and see me again when you have a little less time to spare."

Another great wit was Thomas R. Marshall, Vice President under Woodrow Wilson. He said of himself: "I come from Indiana, the home of more first-rate second-class men than any other state in the Union." It was Marshall, by the way, who coined the phrase, "What this country needs is a good five cent cigar." And may one suppose that it was Mrs. Marshall who followed this with: "What this country needs is a good cigar-extinguisher."

Most Presidents of the United States have found it obligatory to perfect their public speaking ability, but Calvin Coolidge allowed himself to become a symbol for silence. A wit of the times described him as "the still-life of the party." Coolidge hated public appearances, but when he did speak he always said something worth hearing.

In a brief interview with the President of the Bell Telephone Company, he was told that there were nearly as many telephone booths as cars in the United States. Coolidge wasn't impressed. "The motor car manufacturers needn't worry," he said. "People can't show off in telephone booths."

At a certain function where he made an address, a lady came up to him: "Mr. Coolidge," she gushed, "I must tell you how much I enjoyed your talk. I stood up the whole time."

Coolidge looked through her. "So did I, Madam," he said.

And to a similar type of woman, who was placed at his right as guest of honor, he made the same sort of terse reply. "Do you know, Mr. President," she wheedled, "I have made a bet that I can make you talk. I have bet ten dollars with a friend that I can hold you in conversation for five minutes."

"Well," said Coolidge, with an easy shake of the head, "they won!"

Quite the opposite of Calvin Coolidge was President Harding, known as "the Great Handshaker." Introduced to Henry Ford one day, he said: "I believe I have shaken hands with at least twenty-five percent of the American people."

Ford glanced at a "Tin Lizzie," one of his old-fashioned Model T cars, parked nearby.

"And I suppose I have shaken the bones of about half the population of these United States," he said.

Cordell Hull savored in personality a little of Calvin Coolidge. He was a man of few words and refused to believe anything until he saw visible proof.

While travelling with his staff to Scotland where he was to visit King George V at Balmoral Castle, someone pointed to some sheep grazing in the pasture.

"Look at those sheep!" said the friend. "They have just been sheared."

Hull turned his eyes towards the landscape. "You are right," he said. "They have been sheared. But only one side of them as far as I can see."

A side of him well known to all his friends was Hull's devotion to his wife, who was always his earnest preoccupation. At a gathering of personal friends on one occasion, the conversation turned to the subject of the transmigration of souls. Someone asked Hull: "What would you elect to be if you were to leave this world and had to come back to the old planet to work out another existence?"

The answer was spontaneous: "I would choose to be Mrs. Hull's second husband."

Feuding politicians have existed in England since time immemorial. Two notable cases were Gladstone and Disraeli. The vehemence with which they hated each other is emphasized by a couple of references.

Disraeli said of Gladstone: "He is a sophisticated rhetorician, inebriated with the exuberance of his own verbosity . . ."

And Gladstone handled this chastisement with characteristic adroitness. Asked at a public meeting to distinguish between disaster and calamity, both of which he predicted if Disraeli was to continue in office, he said: "If Mr. Disraeli fell into the Thames, that would be a calamity. If someone pulled him out, that would be a disaster."

This bantering and chaffing of politicians continues, and we have it *ad nauseam* during every election. But where are the political wits today? Witticisms more often come from the audience, and are not reported in the papers.

Thomas E. Dewey was campaigning in the Southwest one day when an anonymous member of the audience stole his thunder.

He was expounding on the favorite 1952 campaign theme of the Republican Party. "The Democrats have been too long in power," he is reported to have said. "We must remember that our party system has two wings."

Instantly a voice rapped out, sharp and clear. "And one ain't got no feathers on it!"

Such audience participation is surely better than speaking to a thoroughly dead audience. Adlai Stevenson addressed such a meeting in a Midwestern town. It was a Democratic Party rally and he was disappointed over the turnout.

On the way out of the auditorium he mentioned this to one of his friends when they were descending to the street level in the elevator.

Overhearing Mr. Stevenson's complaint, the operator wished to mollify him.

"Never mind, Mr. Stevenson!" he said in the kindliest way. "The audience tonight was not representative at all. There was nothing but the ragtag and bobtail of the town. Everybody with any sense at all stayed at home."

In taking leave of statesmen and politicians, a sample of President Eisenhower's humor must be given. In a purported conversation with John Foster Dulles during a short cruise in the Presidential yacht, the two men were discussing the anecdote about George Washington's ability to throw a silver dollar across the Potomac—from one shore to the other.

The yacht was passing the point where Washington was supposed to have performed his feat. Dulles is said to have commented that the breadth of the river seemed so great that perhaps the story should be regarded as legendary.

"One thing must be remembered," said Eisenhower. "A dollar went a great deal further in those days than it does now."

... 10

Lecturing Laxity

Artemus Ward, one of the kings of the American lecture platform, traveled all over the world, giving humorous talks in a colloquial style, which might allow him to be called an early Will Rogers. His fame became known far and wide, and wherever he spoke he drew large audiences.

In London he was engaged to speak as an after-dinner entertainment for a certain titled family. When Artemus Ward arrived at the house, the guests were still at dinner and to his amazement he was shown into the servant's hall to await the time of his appearance.

Soon there emerged shrieks of mirth from the kitchen premises, and the diners wondered what it was all about. A little later they marched upstairs to the drawing room where Artemus Ward was to amuse them, and the host did a doubletake as he saw the lecturer putting on his hat and overcoat.

"I've given my performance," he said. "Your servants were very appreciative indeed!"

Doubtless the sarcasm went home quickly, too. Artemus Ward used to tell a good story on himself. He was vacationing in the South, and, wishing to keep in practice, offered to give a series of free talks before the inmates of the local prison. The offer was accepted, but the appearance of Ward was received coolly by the men. He got the impression that they would have preferred to be shooting craps.

Before the second appearance of the lecturer was due, a deputation of prisoners called upon the prison warden.

"We wish to protest against these lectures," said the spokesman. "They are not included in our sentences."

Artemus Ward insisted that there were "talkees" as well as talkers. He said that the perfect talker does not monologue but tries to find the "talkees" in his audience. How few lecturers today understand that secret, only succeeding in putting their audiences to sleep!

Recently there was eloquent proof of this when a so-called celebrity was giving a talk before a women's club on the eastern seaboard. In the middle of it there was a sudden gasp from a member of the audience, and the lecturer saw from his vantage point a lady being assisted out of the auditorium. He continued his talk, but later was given the distressing news that the lady had fractured her jaw yawning!

One of the best speakers of our time was Bernard Shaw who once said that the really successful lecture was that with which everyone disagreed. Public speaking, he insisted in his impish way, requires a sense of histrionics.

He once commented on a speaker whose talk he was reporting next day in the newspaper: "The man spoke well, but had nothing to say. I wish I could print the speaker, for his only merit was in his delivery."

The woes of the lecturer are many. Almost every speaker has met (or been met by) the lady in whose charge he is put before his talk who proceeds to talk *him* to death. Courteous as the lady is obviously trying to be, it is hard lines because the speaker has in front of him the job of talking his audience to life!

Hugh Walpole, the English novelist (who was one of the few good writer-speakers), used to tell a story about such an incident. The good-hearted woman met him at the train upon his arrival.

Her husband sat at the steering wheel as they drove to the auditorium. To begin with, she confused Hugh with Horace Walpole
(who died in 1797). Undaunted, she continued loquaciously.
"Anyhow, I have read one of your books, Mr. Walpole. I have
read your *Sonia* and can quote from it backwards and forwards."

Politely Walpole advised her that the book in question had
been written by another author.

"Dear, dear!" she said. "How could I be so dumb?"

"Stung again, Isabella," quipped the husband from the driver's
seat.

Every lecturer to women's clubs is familiar with the preamble
of the business session. He waits, rather bored, listening to the
discussion of the club's affairs. Stephen Leacock, a very able
speaker, tells this one. He was sitting in the wings awaiting his
cue. A sullen-faced woman was explaining that the finances of the
club were none too good.

"In fact," she said, "due to our low budget, it was thought
we might have to raise the dues. But luckily we have been able
to book some speakers who are very cheap, beginning with Mr.
Stephen Leacock."

Like any other type of artist, a good speaker is capable of a
poor performance. And a talk tailored incorrectly for a given audience can help to bring this calamity about. The noted Irish
dramatist Dr. Lennox Robinson was booked to speak before a
group of Rotarians and their wives in a Chicago suburb. His
name was then famous for a brilliant comedy called *The White-
headed Boy*. But a melancholy exterior hides the workings of his
comic mind. Dr. Robinson looks on the world through the lenses
of thick convex spectacles which give the impression that he is
continually on the verge of tears.

He was met at the train by the wife of the club president. "Dr.
Robinson," she purred, "we are all looking forward to hearing you
this evening. You see, we want to laugh, and you are going to
make us laugh, aren't you?"

Lennox was quick to see that the talk which he had prepared was not going to suit. "I'm going to tell you about the Abbey Theater, Lady Gregory and William Butler Yeats," he pleaded. "I am not a comedian."

But the lady would have none of it. "You've simply got to make us laugh," she persisted.

So Lennox scrapped the more serious poems by Yeats which he planned to read and also jettisoned his excursion into the profound philosophy of Lady Gregory's plays.

That evening his talk fell on very stony soil. Back in New York, his agent said to him: "Something went sour with your talk to the Rotarians out Chicago way. They refuse to pay the fee!"

A similar fiasco occurred when Lord Dunsany came to America to make a lecture tour in 1920. Though a literary artist of superior craftsmanship, Lord Dunsany simply could not understand how to hold an audience then. At New York's Peter Cooper Hall he was sitting on the stage, ready to begin his talk.

Suddenly Lord Dunsany felt a draught of cold air circulating around the back of his neck. Shivering dismally, he called the manager to the edge of the stage and in a stentorian voice asked if anything could be done about it.

"I'm sorry, Lord Dunsany," the man said. "That draught is due to people coming into the hall. The door has to open to let them in."

The great Irish mythologist growled like a bear. Raising himself to his great height, he commenced his talk which was on a very intellectual level, aimed at a scholarly audience. After half an hour of speaking, he shivered again.

"There's that draught again," he bitterly complained. "Where is it coming from now?"

The manager came rushing forward. "I'm sorry," he said ruefully. "This time the draught is coming from the door opening to let people out."

Visiting lecturers from abroad not only often have titles, but sometimes they carry very historical names, too. Such was the case of Sir Walter Raleigh, the eminent English scholar, who came to this country in 1932 to give some talks at universities.

At Yale he was met at the railway station by an official who had no idea of his appearance. The man accosted a dismounting passenger who looked as if he might be Sir Walter, an elderly bearded chap with a high-domed forehead.

"Pardon me, sir," he asked diffidently, "are you Sir Walter Raleigh?"

The passenger turned a morose eye on his questioner: "No, I'm the Earl of Essex. Sir Walter Raleigh is playing whist with Queen Elizabeth in the club car."

Sir Thomas Lipton may not be a venerable name in history but it has a lot to do with the subjects of tea and yachting. The great tea merchant-sportsman came to America on several visits and once found himself in Boston.

A public reception was given where he was honored as one of the participants in the race to win the *America's* Cup yachting trophy. Asked to say a few words, he rose to the occasion beautifully. By way of introduction, he referred to the way in which Boston would always be immortally associated with tea.

"You were quite right to throw the tea into the Bay—because it wasn't Lipton's!"

Sometimes lecturers drink something stronger than tea, which is fatal if they do so before they perform. F. Scott Fitzgerald, the famed American novelist, tried to augment his earnings by lecturing at one time. On one of these occasions he had imbibed a little too freely of *spiritus frumenti*, but managed to get through his rehearsed talk which he had fixed in his memory.

At the close of his talk he received great applause which was probably due as much to his name as a writer as the talk itself. But a hush fell over the group when, at the first break in applause, the speaker began his speech all over again!

Program chairmen are always nervous that something amiss

may happen. Perhaps that is why they usually make such long-winded introductions for speakers and sometimes get their signals crossed.

A story is told about General George C. Marshall who honored a certain women's club with his presence. It was at the time when General Marshall and General Eisenhower were closely associated in the war and the occasion for the club meeting was a patriotic event of one kind or another. After making appropriate references to the national importance of the meeting, the chairman said:

"We all know how busy the General must be, and what a favor he is doing by being with us today. We must not detain him a moment longer than necessary because we know how anxious he is to return to the arms of Mrs. Eisenhower."

Introductions can be unconsciously discourteous. Sir Harry Lauder, the great Scottish comedian, was introduced at a large charity banquet by an inexperienced chairman.

"You have all paid large sums to hear the one and only Sir Harry Lauder," he said. "But if Sir Harry didn't say a word, you would get your money's worth just by the sight of his funny face and bow legs."

The beloved comedian was obviously insulted, yet he concealed his chagrin. "That reminds me," he said by way of reply, "of the time I was touring America. A man on the train kept pressing me to stop over in Chicago so that I could meet his wife. Twice I refused, and the third time I asked him what his reason was.

" 'Well,' drawled the man, 'my wife says that I am the ugliest man in the world and I want her to see you.' "

Then Sir Harry glanced at the Chairman. "You see, I was prompted to tell you this story because the man on the train looked remarkably like my friend over there."

While on the subject of errors in introductions, there was the occasion when the Bishop of London was mistakenly called the Archbishop of Canterbury at a public function which he was about to address. This would not have mattered had not the Archbishop himself been on the platform and was also to speak.

The Bishop handled the situation with calculated charm. He put a hushing finger to his lips, saying: "Not yet! Not yet!"

Such presence of mind in handling an embarrassing situation is a gift. Another divine, Henry Ward Beecher, had it to a fine degree. Once when he was addressing a public gathering not associated with any religious festival, a member of the crowd imitated the crowing of a cock. It was such a good imitation that the audience burst into laughter.

Beecher's solemn subject was interrupted and he knew he must show his disdain. But how? He took his watch out of his pocket and looked at it. "Dear me," he said. "My watch must have stopped. It must be morning instead of afternoon. The instincts of the lower animals are always infallible."

Which was similar to the way in which Charles Lamb extricated himself when giving a talk in which he said more than he wisely should about a certain public figure. There was a loud hiss from a member of the audience. Lamb said calmly: "There are only three things that hiss: a goose, a snake, and a fool . . . Come forth and be identified."

No one responded and the great essayist continued without further unpleasantness.

Bernard Shaw made a good retort to a heckler at one of his lectures. Shaw was holding forth on the merits of the sterling qualities. These qualities, in his opinion, were as rare as geniuses like himself were commonplace.

The heckler argued that genius was indeed rare, whereas nine people out of ten are simple and undistinguished.

"If so," replied G.B.S., "it is the tenth I always have to deal with."

And it is usually the tenth among public men who are good speakers. At least one American President was always seized by an attack of neurotic frenzy every time he got up to make a speech. And Andrew Mellon, the former Ambassador to the Court of St. James, did not seem able to raise his voice above a whisper when he spoke in public.

He was constantly asked to speak louder and on one particular occasion one of his colleagues reminded him about it. After his talk he asked: "Did you hear me all right this time?"

"Well," replied the friend, "at least we *overheard* you."

Mark Twain usually spoke too loudly. But towards the end of his life his voice became thin and reedy. He made his last important speech before an Anglo-American banquet in London. He said: "It is frequently asserted these days that literature is dead. Dickens is dead. Carlyle is dead. Ruskin is dying. And I'm not feeling very well myself tonight."

Mark Twain gave thousands of lectures in America which were always successful. On one occasion he had difficulty in gaining entrance into the auditorium where he was scheduled to speak. He had been mingling with the crowd outside in order to size up his audience. At the door, he nodded to the attendant taking the tickets.

"I'm the speaker tonight," he said.

"Oh, no you don't!" the man snarled unpleasantly. "You're the third fellow with a big hat and moustache who has claimed to be Mark Twain and has tried to get in free."

Questions from the audience often answer what the speaker has said already. Sir James Barrie was a man filled with self-pity, and when he spoke his voice was clothed with a sighing melancholy. Only seldom was he persuaded to give a public address. But the famous author of *Peter Pan* was forced to say a few words when he was accepting an honorary degree at a Scotch University.

Sir James spoke of the hazards of being a playwright, and he said that he felt he had been far more fortunate than he deserved. Afterwards he was introduced to members of the University and a very intense student of playwrighting took the liberty of ask-

ing a question: "Have you any idea why some of your plays have
not been as successful as your *Peter Pan?*"

"Yes. The answer is," said Sir James with eyes twinkling, "that
some of my plays peter out and others pan out."

Speaking before an Anglo-American group in London, Sir
Anthony Eden followed an American speaker who had harped on
the subject of "the American Eagle."

"The American Eagle can spread its wings and fly anywhere
these days," said the speaker. "It has wings such as no other bird
has ever been given . . ."

By way of answer, Sir Anthony said: "In all humility, I would
ask you not to forget that it took a fine old hen to hatch such an
eagle!"

An odd remark was made by the president of an athletic association who was presenting Roger Bannister with a silver goblet.
The speaker said: "You have won this cup by the use of your
legs. Be sure you don't lose your legs by the use of this cup."

Program managers of the American lecture circuit will remember with mixed feelings the visit to the United States of Count
Hermann Keyserling. An exceedingly egotistical man, who had
written several books of empirical philosophy (so personal a type
of philosophy that one critic said: "Count Keyserling has lived
on terms of obscene intimacy with himself"), he made an impact
that will never be forgotten.

By his request his agents sent out a manifesto which needs no
comment:

"The following will help you to understand Count Keyserling's
preferences better than anything else. He is a charming and fascinating guest as long as his wishes are considered, but when they
are disregarded he becomes irritable, and this reacts on his speaking ability.

"The Count dislikes sight-seeing. He never sees anything (sic)
later than six hours before a lecture. He dreads his room being
over-heated. He does not dine before a lecture. However, half an

hour prior to the time he is to speak, he likes to be served a strong cup of coffee and a sandwich of roast beef or chicken (white meat).

"He does not like to meet anyone after his lecture and wishes to leave immediately and be taken to a sit-down supper at which must be served French wines or champagne. The latter is preferable as it helps him to recover from the nervous strain produced by his lecture. But if this cannot be obtained, French claret (vintage year) will do.

"He cannot eat raw fruit, salad or vegetables, excepting potatoes (boiled or mashed). He lives chiefly on fresh fish and oysters on the half-shell, also beef, lamb and white meat of fowl.

"The Count enjoys the society of attractive women."

One is tempted to ask: Did he prefer blondes or brunettes?

... 11

Travelers' Tales

Without a sense of humor, traveling pleasure can be ruined. Equipped with a good one, all unexpected happenings, delays, mistakes of others, and even uncongenial companions can provide endless material for enjoyment. In fine, traveling is always fraught with difficulties and the periods of calm are rare!

Until comparatively recently, travel has been slow. Not so long ago people were creeping overland on coach or horseback—even on foot.

After the war with Mexico was won and California had been ceded to the U.S.A., President Taylor sent Captain W. T. Sherman (later to become famous as an important Confederate general) to inspect the newly acquired territory.

The young captain travelled through the wastelands of the West to cactus-covered California, at that time barely inhabited at all. He heaved a sigh as he set eyes on the void of the Pacific Ocean which brought him to an abrupt halt.

Back in Washington, the President asked him what he thought of the new possession.

"Do you honestly want my opinion, Mr. President?"

"That's why I sent you all that way."

"Well, we're going to have to fight another war!"

159

"Another war? How come, Captain?"

"To make the Mexicans take back California from us. It's not worth a damn!"

Another figure in anecdotal Americana of this period is General McClellan, one of the leaders in the Civil War. He irritated President Lincoln on several occasions because of his headstrong tactics and once sent Lincoln a bulletin which he headed: "Headquarters Saddle."

The President shook his head with annoyance.

"Poor McClellan," he said. "He has his headquarters where his hindquarters ought to be!"

Dr. Samuel Johnson, that most astute of all travelers, hated conveyance on horseback and when he was taken by Boswell by that method of conveyance to see the Giant's Causeway in Ireland, he arrived at the remarkable sight in a disagreeable mood. He gazed at the columnar basalt rock which is considered one of the wonders of the world, and shrugged his great shoulders.

Boswell asked him: "Isn't this worth seeing?"

"Yes," replied the literary king, "worth seeing. But not worth going to see."

Travel stories are always apt to become exaggerated. A man called "Klondike" Mike Mahoney (no relative of mine, as far as I know) won a place in Alaskan fame for his four hundred trek by dog-team and sleigh from the gold fields in the frozen North to the Pacific Coast some years ago. He was engaged on the rather macabre mission of taking to California the body of an Alaskan mayor who wished to be buried in his native San Francisco.

Every newspaper in America carried the story of his amazing trip, stating that "Klondike" Mike suffered starvation en route and was also attacked by wolves.

The intrepid adventurer lodged an objection with the editor of the news syndicate which had carried the story on its wires throughout the country. He was annoyed at some of the inaccuracies of the report.

"Actually," he said, "I wasn't attacked by wolves at all, and I had the good sense to take along plenty of food."

"I don't doubt that at all," said the editor, "but if wolves didn't attack you they ought to have. That's the way the American reading public wanted the story and that's the way they got it!"

Rear Admiral Byrd was continually harassed by stupid questions after he returned from his first trip to the North Pole. At a dinner in his honor one society dowager asked him the trite question:

"Wasn't it awfully cold in the Frozen North?"

To which the Rear Admiral countered: "Yes. So cold that one night I was unable to blow out the candle. The flame was frozen and I had to break it off!"

Americans who travel the high seas usually "change their skies but not their friends," but there is the type of traveler who tries to go European with a vengeance. He does not wish to associate with his own nationality.

Harpo Marx knew exactly how to deal with someone of this sort, you may be sure. He was strolling down the Rue de la Paix one day and spotted an old friend from the States. To his amazement and consternation the man cut him dead. So Harpo stopped in his tracks, reversed his direction and sidled up to the man who was deep in conversation with a Parisian *boulevardier*.

"Well," said Harpo, clutching the man's arm, "There I am! How am I? I haven't seen n yself for weeks!"

Needless to say, the friend broke down and apologized.

Today most travelers prefer to drop from the skies into foreign lands by aeroplane rather than the more gradual transition of an ocean liner. As the Cunard slogan goes: "Getting there is half the fun," and some people do miss a great deal.

Will Rogers used to tell of a trip he took in the "Berengaria." On his way to his cabin one night, a lady passenger stopped him. She had not yet found her sea legs and was looking pale.

"Oh, Mr. Rogers," she said, "I am lost. Will you please help me to find my cabin? It is either on this deck or the one below. I forget the number exactly."

So Rogers wandered about with the unsteady lady, up one corridor and down another. At last he became desperate.

"Are you sure, Madame," he asked, "that your cabin is on this ship?"

Speaking of *mal de mer*, there is a story about President Wilson en route to the Versailles Conference. Aboard the ship was also an aspiring young reporter who was determined to get some "copy" from Wilson.

One morning bright and early he spied him on the top deck all alone, stretched out in a chair wishing that he was back on *terra firma*.

"Mr. President," said the young man, "won't you please make a statement to me for my paper? If you will only say one sentence I could perhaps be promoted to the job of assistant editor."

The President raised himself and with a rolling gait walked to the side of the ship. The young man followed, notebook and pencil ready.

"All right," said Wilson, "as you know, the question of agrarian reform is on the agenda. And you can quote me as saying that I am definitely in favor of a 'back to the land' movement."

President Wilson was capable of excellent repartee. When he was President of Princeton, the son of Anglo-American parents was brought by his mother all the way from England to be entered at the University. The mother was English, the father an American who worked in England and wished his son to have an American education. But the mother was evidently suspicious of Yankee institutions and her attitude implied that she felt she was doing Princeton a favor in sending her son there.

"I suppose," she said to Wilson, "that there is a special spiritual counselor if my son needs one?"

Wilson politely assured her that there was.

"Will you please see that my son's marks are sent to me regularly?"

"Indeed I will, Madam. And if they are not up to standard, we shall return the boy."

President Wilson sent Charles G. Dawes abroad during the war to attend a military conference. A purple-faced English colonel met the Mr. Dawes at the chateau outside of Paris where the meeting was to be held. The American statesman was substituting for General Pershing, who was detained elsewhere. "And where is General Pershing?" asked the colonel haughtily. "It is of the first importance that he should be here."

Dawes was known for his cantankerous nature and forthright manner. "Well, *I'm* here. And here with all his power. Take me to see your superior at once."

Which brings to mind a story they tell about John Gunther in Dublin. He had travelled across the Channel especially to get an interview with Mr. De Valera. Presenting himself to the receptionist at the Dail (Irish Parliament), he said: "I am John Gunther and I have an appointment with Mr. De Valera."

"Take a chair, please," said the receptionist.

"But I haven't much time. Don't you know who I am? My name should be known to you."

"Then take two chairs, please," said the receptionist, firmly.

Alluding to General Pershing inevitably puts one in mind of a great general of our time—George C. Marshall. His name is immortally associated with the Marshall Plan, which has its enthusiasts and its detractors.

The story, which is obviously apocryphal, concerns the President of Andorra, the smallest republic in the world. The little man came all the way to Washington in order to see the General about getting an allotment of funds from the Plan for his country.

After putting his request as eloquently as he was able, General Marshall asked: "Do you have any Communists in your country?"

The President answered with alacrity. "No, sir, not one single Communist as far as I know."

"Then I am very sorry. The Marshall Plan can do nothing for you. It is designed only to help Communist-infested countries."

Much crestfallen, the little man went home. In his office, on the first morning of his return, he telephoned to the President of the country adjacent to his. "Can you let me have some Communists, please," he pleaded, "so that I can get some money out of the Marshall Plan?"

"Sorry," said the President. "Our Communists are all busy."

Ernest Bevin, the British Foreign Minister, travelled to Greece and used to tell this story. He was invited to a ball given by the King and Queen at Athens. Apparently the royal couple were very democratic and their knowledge that the Minister was a Laborite impelled them to ask some of the laboring ranks.

Mr. Bevin hired a limousine to take him to the Palace and was rather surprised to receive a telephone call at his hotel from the chauffeur. "Would you mind starting a little early, please, as I happen to be going to the ball myself," the man said. "And I have to get home to change my clothes."

Later, Mr. Bevin noted that the chauffeur was waltzing with the Queen herself!

Travelers usually find that a little knowledge of the foreign language is almost as bad as none at all. When Monsieur Tardieu, the French Prime Minister, went to London he took along with him only enough English to survive. But when he made a speech, he floundered badly. He began by saying: "Gentlemen I am pleased to be here; and Ladies, I am very 'appy to be in your middle."

Misapprehensions occur even when travelers don't have to speak the language. One of the American robber barons, Jay Gould, went abroad to France for the first time when his daughter, Anna, was to marry the famed French *litterateur* and *raconteur*, Boni de Castellane. Gould's future son-in-law spoke English perfectly and was very knowledgeable about French history. When showing him the sights, he pointed to a newly unveiled statue of Charlemagne. Describing at length the feats of this remarkable French King, he did not know that Mr. Gould's mind was a complete blank on the subject.

Later that day, Jay Gould got up enough courage to ask a question: "Tell me more about this Charley Maine. He sounds like an Englishman."

Returning home aboard a first class liner, Mr. Gould mistook the Captain for a steward. Pointing proudly to his braid, the Captain said to him: "If you think I'm a steward, what on earth do you think the Captain should look like?"

Which reminds me of a story told aboard a famous liner. On one of her voyages, the personal physician to King George V was traveling to New York. Since Lord Dawson of Penn has since gone to his reward, it may be permissible to quote an amusing piece of doggerel about him which is, of course, devoid of truthful foundation:

Lord Dawson of Penn,
Has killed many men.
That's why we sing
God save the King!

The scene shifts to the Turkish bath aboard the ship where Lord Dawson was relaxing after a massage. A page entered the bath-house and announced that Lord Dawson of Penn was being sought by the purser, evidently on some important matter. The superintendent of the baths felt sure that the drowsing patient could not possibly be the eminent physician and jokingly quoted the doggerel verse already given.

The recumbent figure of Lord Dawson slowly raised itself off the massage table and indignantly stalked off to the dressing room. There was no doubt now in the mind of the superintendent to whom the figure belonged! And he soon found his sea duties at an end.

They say tourists go to London in order to see the Changing of the Guard—and nowadays they go to Paris to see the changing of the Government! Edouard Herriot remains the President of the French Assembly, the dean among French statesmen. Some years ago I went to interview him at an ancient little walled city called Pérouges, in the Department of Ain. Here he spends his summers and is permanently President for the Preservation of Pérouges, which is, incidentally, an antiquarian's paradise. Herriot is now almost as old as Pérouges, but at one time his name was associated with many a beautiful Frenchwoman.

While escorting me round the city (which took about ten minutes), an attractive American woman passed on her own tour of inspection. Herriot sighed, gazed back at her lingeringly and said, "If only I were seventy-five again!"

Travelers to Ireland who like literature will want to see the statue of Thomas Moore near College Green and which stands next to a public convenience. At the time this statue was erected there was a slight controversy. Many of the poet's admirers thought that it should have a more felicitous setting. Tim Healy drew a good laugh with his comment: "What better association for the author of *The Meeting of the Waters?*"

The English counterpart of Tim Healy is the philosopher C. E. M. Joad, who equalled the Irishman's reputation for wit and humor. He came to the United States only once and wrote a sarcastic book about America, called *The Babbit Warren*. But one experience he had in the States he did not include, but saved it to tell *a haut voix* to his friends.

It seems he was being escorted through one of the major motor-car factories in Detroit, where even the human element appears like automata. Dazzled with so many mechanical operations, he was taken to the restaurant, where even the food was served automatically.

On the way out of the factory, Dr. Joad was descending in the elevator with his escort when one of the factory hands, also a passenger, pinched a female passenger in the usual place. The young woman reacted indignantly. But Dr. Joad rejoiced.

"Thank God," he cried, "that something is done by hand in this factory!"

While on the subject of factory methods, there is a story told in Detroit about the visit paid by Governor Mennen Williams of Michigan to one of the large motorcar companies. In his honor an entire automobile was put together in the record time of ten minutes. This staggering piece of manufacturing was given wide publicity and one day an official of the company received a telephone call from an irate member of the public.

"Is it true that you put together a motorcar in ten minutes last month?"

"Yes, indeed. It was done in the presence of Governor Williams himself."

"I don't give a damn for whom it was done. It was my bad luck to get that car and I'm going to make you exchange it."

When about to embark on a tour abroad, Will Rogers had an interview with President Franklin D. Roosevelt.

"I've got a commission for you, Will," he said.

"Anything to help pay my fare?"

"Yes. I'm going to authorize you to collect the war debts in England, France, Italy and Germany. Now begin with Mussolini . . ."

"And how much do I get?"

"Oh, I'm putting you on a commission basis, Will."

"No thanks," said Will very wisely, "I'd rather take a job as a Chinese coolie!"

Will once said that he would prefer heaven as a climate, but hell for company, because most of his friends were bound to go there.

Pertinent to this witticism is a spurious story about an American woman who was discussing a European voyage with a clerk at a travel bureau. The man happened to be Irish and naturally enough he urged the woman to include Ireland on her itinerary. But the lady was disinclined.

"No," she said firmly. "I am told that Ireland is cold and damp and full of Catholics."

"Well, Madam," said the clerk with tongue in cheek. "You'd better go to hell, for there it's warm and dry—and full of Protestants."

Ireland has a lure for the traveler, and for those who plan to go there it is as well to prime themselves first with a little history of the country. As one travels through the miles of Irish bog and sees the battered ruins, so eloquent of past glories, there is a suggestion of ancient Greece. Bing Crosby got into conversation with a gaffer over there and exhibited his ignorance of Irish history. The man questioned him thus, not at all impressed that he was talking to Hollywood's most popular idol:

"Have you ever heard of the Battle of the Boyne?"

"No, I haven't."

"Of Derry Wall?"

"No."

"Of Newtownbutler?"

Bing shrugged his shoulders negatively, and the gaffer looked him belligerently in the eyes.

"Ach, man!" he said. "Go home and read your Bible!"

It is not generally known that Baron Münchhausen, the world traveler and teller of tall tales, died in Ireland. The erratic German scholar (whose real name was Rudolf Raspe) is buried at Muckross, on the shore of that famous lake in Killarney. He invented many a good tale about the Irish and one of them offers a good specimen of Irish vituperation.

It concerns the Irishman who wants to go to Connemara, that wild and desolate haven which is the spiritual home of the Irish exile, where there is no destination, only pauses—to admire the scenery. The man was in his cabin packing his things and a friend came to say goodbye to him.

"Where are you going?" asked the friend.

"I'm going to Connemara."

"You mean you're going to Connemara, God willing?"

"No! I'm going to Connemara, God willing or not!"

And for that piece of heresy the man was changed into a frog and relegated to a pond for a number of years. Eventually, after due penance, the man was allowed to regain his mortal shape, and he returned to his home, and began packing up his things again.

The same friend came to say farewell, and a conversation ensued:

"Where are you going this time?" he asked.

"I'm going to Connemara," said the man, his eyes glaring.

"You mean you're going to Connemara, God willing?"

"No," shouted the would-be traveler. "I'm going to Connemara, or back to the frog-pond."

On a recent trip to Ireland, I picked up a Münchhausen type of story. I was visiting one of the Aran Islands which lie off the Coast of Galway—truly symbols of human conquest, for the Irish live there with the barest necessities of life. In these beautiful islands, superstition still governs the lives of the natives. They believe they can see phantom ships that pass in the night and on certain clear days they insist that the mythical island, Hy Brasil, after which Brazil got its name, is visible.

One particular superstition lays down that the seal is a sacred creature, that it is tantamount to murder to kill a seal. Conversing with a local gaffer, I was informed that the leading family, which is named McConmora (translated into English it is MacNamara), is actually descended from a seal.

It seems that the founder of this family was strolling around the island many hundreds of years ago, and came across a beautiful seal. Suddenly, before his affrighted eyes, the seal changed into a beautiful woman and proposed marriage to the man. He accepted and thus the family of McConmora was founded.

Naturally enough I thought my friend was kidding me along. "Do you really believe this amazing story?" I asked, smiling broadly.

The gaffer's face colored like a ripe apple and he assumed a manner of earnestness.

"No," he replied, "I can't say I really believe the story. But I must admit that the McConmoras are all born with very short arms."

There is actually an Irish family whose coat of arms is adorned with three mallards. Samuel Foote met the head of the house in Dublin at the Kildare Street Club.

"I'm told your coat of arms is decorated with three ducks," he said. "And I suggest your motto should be 'Quack! Quack! Quack!' "

Which brings to mind the favorite story cited to illustrate the old theory called "Bow-wow" which asserts that our prehistoric ancestors imitated certain sounds to distinguish the objects they wished to designate.

An Englishman travelling in the Orient was being entertained at dinner by a Chinaman. He was anxious to know what the dish of food placed before him was, and neither being acquainted with each other's language, he raised the cover and inquired politely:

"Quack-quack?"

Upon which the Chinaman, smiling blandly, shook his Oriental head and wished to communicate that the dish was a stew made of a Chinese canine called a Chow. So he merely said: "Bow-wow."

In China the formality of knocking on a bedroom door is not always heeded. Hence, when Margot Asquith, the wife of Prime Minister Herbert Asquith, was staying in Hong Kong, the Chinese manservant entered without any sound.

"I wish you would knock before you enter my room," said Lady Asquith angrily. "You might come in one time and find me undressed."

"Oh, no, Missy," grinned the servant. "I always look through the keyhole first."

Which smacks a little of the tactful English butler who entered the bathroom of a houseguest and found a lady bathing. He made his exit with the perfect excuse: "Pardon me, sir!"

When the celebrated Chinese writer Lin Yutang visited Hilaire Belloc in England, the two men took walks along the country lanes. The Chinaman was fond of quoting Confucius and on one of these outings a fierce dog appeared from nowhere, growling at Belloc. The great writer became alarmed and could not conceal his fright from Lin Yutang.

"Never fear," said Lin Yutang consolingly, "Confucius says barking dog never bites."

"That's nice to hear," said Belloc nervously, "but does the dog know the proverb?"

Crossing back to Ireland again, there is a wild beast which roams the countryside known as the Irish Bull. This rapacious animal has been described as "a male animal which is always pregnant." For an Irish Bull is a blunder in speech wherein one can always say more than one can otherwise.

The traveler will find it rewarding to keep his eyes and ears alerted for this interesting creature. Not long ago Mr. John A. Costello, the new Prime Minister, manufactured a good one: "Thank God, the bridge has broken down which has so long separated the English and the Irish people."

And traveling through the country, I noticed a sign in a river bed, where people apparently were used to ford when sufficiently shallow: "If this sign is invisible, this river is unsafe to cross."

And a notice hung in a Government office: "Anyone having no business in this office will please finish it as soon as possible."

Advertisements are sometimes a good source. In a country town newspaper I saw this one regarding a lost dog: "Terrier, which answers to the name of Pat. Age not known but looks older than he is."

One should add that traveling in Ireland is leisurely. The Irish are a contemplative race and dislike to hurry. Once when I was traveling to Cork City from Dublin I asked if the train left on time (very few of them do!).

"Yes," said the stationmaster, "and it's a great inconvenience to the traveling public."

Thackeray once took a trip to Ireland, and wrote interestingly about the country in his *Irish Sketch Book*. He tells in that book about the beggars who were, in the days of which he wrote, rampant in the cities and famous for their scathing wit if you happened to pass them by.

One day Thackeray was walking along St. Patrick Street in Cork City and a woman sidled up to him: "May God follow ye! May God follow ye!" the old crone kept saying.

But Thackeray paid no attention. He reached into his pocket for his handkerchief and when the beggar realized that she would get nothing from him, she flung an antidote to her benediction: "And may He never overtake ye!"

The next time Thackeray met a persistent mendicant he had made up his mind to be polite, but he was still firm in his attitude to save his charity for other causes. In Dublin he passed a woman selling thread.

"Buy a little thread and help a poor old lady," she said pathetically.

"Sorry, I don't sew," said Thackeray, very apologetically.

"And neither shall ye reap," said the old woman, spitting poison.

Thackeray noted that Irish epitaphs sometimes are found to mirror the social pattern of the times when humor was uppermost in the land. I have come across a few worth noting here in my travels in the Emerald Isle, the first of which was inscribed on the tombstone of a locally-known undertaker's wife:

> Here lies my wife,
> Here let her lie.
> She is at peace,
> And so am I!

Another amusing epitaph was placed on the tomb of a house-keeper employed by the notorious Captain Boycott (whose name added a word to the English language). Evidently he had more humor than has been credited to him, for he burst into doggerel:

> This stone was laid by Sara's Lord,
> Not Sara's virtues to record.
> For they're well-known to all the town.
> This stone was laid to keep her down!

Religious Revelling

One of the best stories Mark Twain told about himself was about the time when he was lecturing in a small American city and was being introduced by a local preacher. The good-hearted man began asking guidance and forgiveness for everyone present, naming them separately. Finally he wound up with: "Oh, Lord, we have with us a great American humorist. Help us to understand what he is about to say, and please, Lord, make us laugh as much as possible."

Church dignitaries have the reputation for seldom laughing, but in the past there was a prevalance of wit amongst them. By far the best specimens come from that irrepressible and delightful Reverend Sydney Smith (1771-1845).

At a meeting of the Dean and Chapter of St. Paul's Cathedral in London, he was advised that a new wooden pavement was needed in a section of the great edifice.

After carefully surveying the floor in need of repair, he said: "My dear fellows, all you have to do is to put your heads together and the thing is done."

This delicious piece of fun was shortly followed by another. At a tea party in his honor his hostess was trying to force an extra cup of tea on him. Reverend Smith was fond of strong tea which he described as "a civil and wakeful drink," but in this instance the tea was very weak indeed.

"Just one more cup, Reverend Sir," said the lady.

"No thank you," said Smith, frankly. "My back teeth are already under water."

When told that a professional fighter of note had decided to become a preacher, he commented: "Let us hope he will continue to put them to sleep."

And once when saying his prayers, which he always did out loud, he was overheard to say: "Now Lord, I'll tell you an anecdote."

Anecdotes galore are told about Henry Ward Beecher who, like Reverend Sydney Smith made friends with all faiths. Riding in a streetcar (horse-drawn in those days, of course), some juvenile delinquents of the day were scoffing at religion and making unpleasant references to his clerical garb.

As Dr. Beecher left the vehicle, he spoke to the boys for the first time. "We shall meet again soon."

One of the boys asked, very rudely, "Where?"

"You see," said Beecher, "I am the visiting chaplain in several of the prisons in this district."

Which is a little like the story told about Cardinal Newman. He was traveling in a railway carriage and sitting opposite were a couple of men who made continual and derogatory remarks about the Church. The Cardinal said not a word until one of the men came to his destination. Getting out of the train, the Cardinal called him back. "Here! You've forgotten something!"

The man turned round quickly. "Have I left something behind?"

"Yes," said the Cardinal, "a very bad impression!"

Henry Ward Beecher used to tell a delightful story about himself. Walking through the streets of Brooklyn, he ran into a crowd of boys sitting in a circle with a small dog in the center.

"What are you doing with that dog?" asked Beecher.

"Well, sir," answered the smallest lad, "it's like this. We're having a competition. Whoever tells the biggest lie gets the dog."

"Surely none of you lie?" asked the kindly clergyman. "When I was a boy of your age, I never told a lie."

A deprecatory grin came over the face of one of the youngsters. "Hand him the dog, boys," he cried.

Beecher's great and good friend Thoreau was an influence upon American thought of that time and, to some extent, still influences a circumscribed circle of admirers. When speaking once about the superiority of one religion over another, he summed it up neatly. "No matter what our faith, we are all members of the human race. And can one say worse?"

At one of his talks on philosophy, a gushing lady spoke up: "Tell me, please, what is your opinion of the mystery of life?"

Slowly, ponderously, Thoreau answered: "Life, Madam, is the predicament which precedes death."

Yet this great American was intensely religious. Once, when lying very ill, a clergyman asked him: "Have you made your peace with God?"

Quietly, the great man replied: "I didn't know that God and I had ever quarreled."

Thoreau knew that if life is to be rounded and many-colored, like the rainbow, both joy and sorrow must come to it. Those who never know anything but prosperity and pleasure must become hard and shallow. Take the case of the man who had been studying some newfangled religion, stressing the materialistic side of human happiness. He became so dazzled with the slap-happy philosophy that he finally committed suicide leaving a note behind: "I'm tired of being so damned happy!"

When Margaret Fuller, the American writer, felt the fingers of doubt, she went to see Carlyle. She told him she was sorely worried because she could not think out a satisfactory explanation of the universe. In short, she was victimized by nineteenth century materialistic thought.

So the great Carlyle tried his gentle suasion on her. He told her that our poor minds are finite and that she was toying with infinite questions. "You can't explain the universe," he said, "unless you are able to step outside of it."

Later someone told him that Miss Fuller had decided he was right. And she herself sent him a message: "I accept the universe," she said.

Carlyle made only one comment. "My Gad, she'd better!"

Crackpots have, from time to time, predicted the end of the world. When Emerson heard of one who had predicted the end of the world in a few days' time, he said: "Good! We'll get on very well without it, won't we?"

It took the fine mind of Lewis Carroll to prove that perfect nonsense could only be produced by a trained logician. He was actually a mathematician of high rank, and if one reads *Alice in Wonderland* carefully, one soon realizes that it was written in terms of abstract mathematics. Sardonic humour was Carroll's speciality. After church one Sunday he departed with his friend the Vicar, who had given a dull sermon. Rain was falling and Lewis Carroll offered the Vicar part coverage of his umbrella, but he made a gesture of refusal. "I don't mind a little wet," he said.

"You were certainly dry enough in church today," was Carroll's sarcastic shaft.

Carroll's *Alice in Wonderland* is almost as satirical as Swift's *Gulliver's Travels* which teems with devastating attacks on all the important men of the times. As one wanders about the streets of Dublin which resounded with his sparkling wit, or in the lanes and alleys where the people shouted his praise, one hears echoes of his unexampled popularity.

A story is told in Dublin which is little known to his devotees. One day he was sheltering himself under a tree during a storm and along came a young couple who took cover beside him. Seeing that the stranger wore a clergyman's attire, they told him that they were on their way to get married.

"I'll marry you here and now," said the great Dean of Saint Patrick's Cathedral. And what's more he did it in verse, extemporaneous and witty:

> In stormy weather
> I join these two together.
> Let none but He who rolls the thunder,
> Part this man and woman asunder.

At one time he was the incumbent of a quiet little village named Laracor in Ireland, where he used to preach to a small congregation. Even there he had a reputation for being eccentric. One day a small boy called upon him: "May I see the bats which my mother says you keep in the belfry?" the child asked him.

It may have been Swift who was asked by some cheeky person: "Can you tell me the way to heaven?"

"Certainly," replied Swift, "turn to the right and keep straight on."

Even the Archbishop of Canterbury has to deal with impertinent people occasionally. The venerated prelate was giving a talk in London, in the course of which he observed: "It is said that the road to hell is paved with good intentions. But these days, it seems to me, it is paved with wine, women and motorcars."

Voice from the crowd: "Then the sting of death is gone!"

Thanks to this Archbishop, England has been spared a certain amount of scenery desecration. He it was who initiated a campaign against advertising signs. This was aided by such slogans as "I think that I shall never see a road-sign lovely as a tree." And the Archbishop penned a little verse which also helped. Referring to those who, for commercial reasons, ruin the aesthetic pleasures of others, he wrote:

> They play about with works of God,
> And make them seem uncommon odd.

Yet religious maniacs can also mar the scenery, and one sees, often enough, writing on rock formations such as "The sea is His and He made it" near the great sights of Nature. Under one of these I once saw a subtle retaliation: Below the tract was written: "The rocks were yours and you ruined them."

Turning to unorthodox religion, was there ever a more colorful figure among the evangelists than Aimee Semple MacPherson? Constantly at war with the devil, this clever woman insisted that she had given him many an uppercut! She would use every ruse she could think of to interest her followers in religion. Once she appeared on the stage of her temple dressed in the uniform of a speed-cop, riding a real motorcycle.

"I arrest you all in the name of God," she cried. And she proceeded to hand out tickets of arrest to members of the audience.

Aimee became estranged from her mother, but finally they made up. It was at Christmas, so Aimee had her mother delivered to her as a Christmas gift. The poor old lady emerged from a huge brown paper package in which she had been wrapped—gasping and almost on the verge of fainting!

Billy Sunday, the same sort of evangelist, used similar tactics. In one of his revival meetings he requested all the couples present who had never quarreled to come before him. A motley number of couples appeared before him, and Billy held his hands over their heads, as if about to make a benediction. "God bless these damned liars," he said.

Billy Graham carries on in the tradition of Billy Sunday. At a large public meeting in London he asked all those to stand up who were trying to live the life which would get them to heaven. A lot of people got up on their feet, but there was one little man in the front row who remained seated.

"What's the matter with you?" he asked. "Don't you wish to go to heaven?"

Billy's exhaltation was suddenly broken off and there was complete silence. "Not immediately," said the man with an air of conviction.

A story is told about Billy Graham in Scotland where he received his greatest acclaim. He was staying at an Edinburgh hotel and one morning at breakfast he was delighted to hear the strains of "Onward, Christian Soldiers" coming from the lips of the cook in the kitchen. Softly he tiptoed to the door and said a few words to her by way of felicitation.

"Oh," said the Scotswoman, "I always sing that hymn when I boil the eggs. Three verses for soft and five for hardboiled."

Billy Graham did not meet with the unanimous success in France which he had enjoyed in other lands, perhaps because he could not speak French. A similar failure met the Bishop of London who went to the French battlefront during World War I, and was asked to address the French soldiers. His French was of the fractured kind, but he was determined to say a few words by way of benediction. Naturally enough he thought that the word for bless in French would be *blessé*—which of course it is not. He stumbled along as best he could, not making much French, and wound up with "Soyez-vous tout blesserais!" (which means, "Go and get yourselves wounded").

According to the local grapevine, Dr. Norman Vincent Peale was wounded mentally, at least on one occasion. A drunken young man addressed the author of *The Power of Positive Thinking*: "I want to know," he lisped, "what is the difference between positive and negative thinking?"

Dr. Peale was very polite. "Young man," he is supposed to have answered, "if you will ask me that when you are sober, I shall be happy to tell you."

"That's the trouble," the young man mouthed. "When I'm sober I just don't give a damn."

The famous Dr. Peale is, by his own avowal, a salesman. He sells God, a praiseworthy occupation. A man named Prophet Jones calls his form of faith, which has grown into a large organization, "The House of God." This colorful Negro minister has done so well selling God that he is able to live in fabulous luxury.

When the Prophet went to London recently he took an entire floor at the expensive Dorchester House Hotel in Park Lane, arriving with a large suite of assistants. After the first week of his stay he paid his bill with a check signed by himself over the imprint of "The House of God," but due to a technical error the check was returned by the bank to the hotel management. A witty bank-clerk had written on it: "Refer to Maker."

And as soon as this was done, the Prophet cleared up the misunderstanding and the check was paid!

Another terse witticism in this area is attributed to Calvin Coolidge, whose pithy rhetoric we have encountered before. Upon returning from church on a Sunday that his wife had been unable to accompany him, he was asked what the minister had talked about.

"Sin," replied the President.

"But what did he *say?*" quizzed Mrs. Coolidge impatiently.

"He's against it." And with that, he retired behind his newspaper.

Pope Pius IX was a man with a keen sense of humor and many good stories testify to it. He was known for the informality of his audiences when he would engage members in conversation and occasionally cause a ripple of laughter with his humor. Once he spoke to a very fat Englishman.

"What brings you to Rome?" asked His Holiness.

"Faith, Your Holiness! Faith!"

"Well," replied the Pope, "they say that faith can move mountains, so you have come to the right place."

Another time an American woman said to him:

"I must tell Your Holiness that I paid five hundred dollars for a pair of your old socks to cure my arthritis."

"And did they help you?"

"Oh, yes indeed," said the pilgrim, "I never had arthritis again in my life!"

"Interesting," replied the Pope. "I can assure you that they never helped me. My arthritis is as bad as ever!"

It seems incredible that an American gangster was received in audience by a Pope, but it is a fact that the notorious "Bugsie" Siegel was not only received at the Vatican, but was also decorated by the Pope!

It all began with a certain Contessa de Frasso, an American leader of Café Society, who first introduced "Bugsie" to Prince Umberto, who in turn arranged an audience with his father, the King of Italy. It followed as a matter of course that the Pope would also receive anyone as distinguished as "Bugsie" seemed to be.

And so the audience with His Holiness was arranged, during which a minor decoration was pinned on the gangster. After the brief ceremony, a Vatican official had the (rather late) good sense to look up "Bugsie" Siegel in the dossiers, and to his horror he found that this man who had been honored by His Holiness was not the sort of person who ought to receive anything, let alone an audience or a minor decoration from a Pope of Rome.

Something had to be done immediately. Orders were given a Papal messenger to go to "Bugsie" Siegel's hotel and demand the decoration from him.

The emissary arrived just in time to find "Bugsie" preening himself in the mirror at his hotel suite.

"What do you want?" he asked sharply, annoyed at being disturbed.

"I'm sorry, Mr. Siegel," said the emissary, "I must ask you for the return of that medal. There has been an error . . ."

"And whose error?" demanded "Bugsie," discourteously.

Meekly, almost apologetically, the man murmured: "It was an error of His Holiness . . ."

"Bugsie" took another look at himself in the mirror, then turned sharply to the emissary: "It is impossible for the Pope to make an error. He is infallible."

He kept the medal.